MW00649074

Baking Low-Carb

Tasty Sugar-Free Desserts, Cookies, Candies and Breads

By
Diana Lee
Barrington, Illinois

This cookbook is a product of
*Cookbooks by Morris Press **Type 'N $ave**™ program.*
All recipes were typed by the customer.

Printed in the U.S.A. by

P.O. Box 2110 • Kearney, NE 68848

For information on having your cookbook printed, write for
our FREE information packet or call Toll-Free at 1-800-445-6621.

29063 j   1

Before You Begin

Baking low carb is somewhat different than regular baking. You will find that things bake faster and must be watched carefully so they don't become burned or dried out from over baking. Baking with dark bakeware absorbs more heat and may cause foods to cook faster. Dark pans can make breads burn on the outside before the inside is done.

Storing low carb baked goods is also a new ball game. For the most part you will want to keep them in the refrigerator or freezer to prolong their shelf life. If you choose to warm them a little before eating, you may zap them in the microwave but be sure it is for a very short time as again you may dry the food out.

Specific ingredients are called for in my recipes...any substitutes can change the flavor and texture of your recipe.

The ingredients you will be using to bake lowcarb can be difficult to find if you don't have a health food store, a GNC store or grocery store that deals in health food products. I will give you some phone numbers and Internet sights that carry these products. When purchasing any ingredients to use while cooking or baking low carb be sure to read labels and choose the one with the lowest carb count.

Ingredients to have on hand, before you begin, are as follows:

Oat flour can be found in the health food section of your grocery store or at some health food stores. You may also order from Walnut Acres at 1-800-433-3998 or http://www.walnutacres.com/ an Internet site.

High Gluten flour or Vital Wheat Gluten is not to be confused with regular gluten flour; it is a wheat flour with starch removed. Read the label and make sure you are getting a gluten flour that is 75% protein with only 6 grams of carbohydrates per 1/4 cup. This can be found in the health food section or bread flour section of your grocery store or at some health food stores. You may also order from Bakers Catalogue at 1-800-827-5836 or shop KingArthurFlour.com.

Nuts. An economical place to order nuts for baking is Nuts for U at 800-688-7482 or http://www.nuts4u.com an Internet site.

Peanut Butter should be the natural unsweetened kind with only 6 carbs per two tablespoons.

Liquid sweetener. I mention Sweet & Low as that one is usually the easiest to find at your local grocery store and I use the liquid because it doesn't have any carbohydrates. Also, you will find that combining two different kinds of sweeteners will give you a better taste. Heavy whipping cream is just that and can be found in the dairy section. Not to be confused with the whipping cream that is already whipped and has sugar added.

Xanthan gum is used to thicken and is a fiber so doesn't count as a carbohydrate. This can be found at some health food stores or call for catalog or to order at Gluten-free Pantry 800-291-8386 or check their internet site at http://www.glutenfree.net/.

Baking cocoa is found in the spice and baking section of your grocery store. Choose the one with the lowest carb count on the package.

Splenda is a new product used for sweetening that as of this writing was not available in the grocery store but soon will be. For now you can buy it at Low Carb Connoisseur at 864-224-0296 or at http://www.lowcarbconnoisseur.com their Internet ordering site. I can also be ordered at Internet site http://www.splenda.com/. The advantage of this sweetener is that it can be used in baking without losing its sweetening power and is the best tasting of all the sweeteners. You could probably use a baking product like Sugar Twin in place of Splenda but you will definitely not get as good a flavor.

Vanilla Whey Protein Powder is actually a protein drink. GNC stores sell the one I use and the carb counts in the recipes are based on using this. It has 7 carbs per cup of powder and 92 protein per cup. To find a store nearest you, you can check their Internet site at http:www/gnc.com/. CarbSmart carries Designer Whey Protein and can be found at http://www.carbsmart.com or 877-279-7091. Health Kick carries Optimum Nutrition 100% Whey Protein at 888-965-5425 or their Internet site http://www.healthkick.net/index.htm.

Extracts and spices can be found in your grocery store, however sometimes it is difficult to find the more exotic extracts so these you can order from Spices, etc. 800-827-6373 to place an order or order their catalog or their Internet site http//:www.spicesetc.com.

Zucchini. If you have fresh, I would suggest you use it. If it is out of season and you have a problem finding it, you can use the frozen sliced. Measure 2 cups of slices and partially thaw; then place in your food processor and chop.

Table of Contents

Pies & Pastry

My Favorite Recipe

_____

_____

_____

_____

_____

_____

_____

_____

_____

_____

_____

_____

_____

_____

_____

_____

_____

_____

_____

_____

Pies

CHERRY RASPBERRY CUSTARD PIE

³/₄ c. frozen unsweetened cherries (thawed)
½ c. frozen unsweetened raspberries (thawed)
½ tsp. xanthan gum
½ tsp. cinnamon
1 tsp. liquid sweetener Sweet & Low

4 eggs
½ c. water
½ tsp. xanthan gum
1 c. heavy whipping cream
½ c. splenda
2 tbl. liquid sweetener Sweet & Low

Combine cherries, raspberries, ½ tsp. xanthan gum, cinnamon, and 1 tsp. liquid sweetener; mix and set aside. Beat eggs, water, xanthan gum, whipping cream, splenda, and sweetener. In a Pam sprayed 9" pie dish spread the fruit mixture and then pour custard over the top. Bake at 350°for 35 - 45 minutes until set and lightly brown. See index for crust recipe if you wish to use a crust.

Recipe Note: 63 carbohydrates and 15 protein. Does not include crust.

CHOCOLATE PEANUT BUTTER PIE

1 baked nut pie crust (see index)
1 pkg. sugar free instant chocolate pudding
³/₄ c. whipping cream

³/₄ c. water
2 tbl. unsweetened peanut butter
½ c. heavy whipping cream
2 tsp. splenda

Mix water and heavy whipping cream together. Add pudding mix and peanut butter and stir. In another bowl whip ½ c. whipping cream and splenda till stiff. Fold into pudding mixture and pour into a nut crust. See index for crust recipe. Refrigerate.

Recipe Note: Total recipe 78 carbohydrates and 13 protein. This includes pie crust.

COCONUT PIE

4 eggs
1 c. water
1 c. whipping cream
1 c. splenda
2 tsp. liquid sweetener Sweet & Low

¼ c. melted butter
2 tsp. vanilla
¼ c. oat flour
½ tsp. xanthan gum
1¼ c. unsweetened coconut

Beat eggs, water, whipping cream, splenda, sweetener, butter, vanilla, oat flour and gum; beating as you go. Stir in coconut. Pour into a greased 9 inch pie plate. Bake at 350° for 30 - 40 min until set and lightly brown. Chill before serving.

Recipe Note: Total recipe 72 carbohydrate and 18 protein.

CUSTARD PECAN PIE

1 unbaked pie shell (see index)
1 c. Pecan pieces
2 tbl. butter melted
¼ tsp. caramel extract
¼ tsp. vanilla extract
2 tbl. splenda
¼ tsp. cinnamon
4 eggs
½ c. water

¾ c. whipping cream
1 c. splenda
2 tsp. liquid sweetener Sweet & Low
1 tsp. molasses
1 tsp. vanilla extract
2 tsp. maple extract
½ tsp. cinnamon
½ tsp. xanthan gum

Prepare nuts first: In a bowl melt 2 tbl of butter; then, stirring after each addition, add 2 tbl of splenda, caramel and vanilla extract ¼ tsp. cinnamon and pecans. Microwave for 30 seconds; stir. Microwave another 30 seconds; stir, but keep an eye on them so they don't burn...set aside to cool off. Prepare filling: Beat eggs, water, whipping cream, splenda, sweetener, molasses, vanilla extract, maple extract. cinnamon, and gum. Set aside and prepare pie crust. See index for pie crust recipe. Pour filling into crust, sprinkle nuts on top and bake at 350° for 30 to 40 min. until set and lightly brown. Chill before serving. Keep in refrigerator.

Recipe Note: Total recipe 96 carbohydrates and 82 protein.

290631-99

FRESH STRAWBERRY PIE

1 Baked Pie shell (see index)
¾ tsp. Kool Aid Strawberry
  drink mix
1¾ c. boiling water

1 c. Splenda
2 tsp. xanthan gum
1 quart of fresh strawberries

Mix together Kool Aid aid, boiling water, splenda and gum. Let cool to room temperature. Rinse and cut up strawberries and then add to Kool Aid aid mixture when cooled. Pour into a pie shell and refrigerate.

Recipe Note: Total carbohydrates 74 and 71 protein. This includes pie crust.

LEMON RICOTTA CHEESE PIE

1 unbaked pie crust (see index)
1 15 oz. container Ricotta Cheese
4 eggs, separated
¼ c. splenda
1½ tsp. liquid sweetener Sweet &
  Low

½ tsp. lemon extract
½ tsp. vanilla extract
1½ tbl. lemon peel
¼ tsp. cream of tartar

Beat ricotta, egg yolks, splenda and sweetener till blended. Add lemon extract, vanilla extract and lemon peel; mix. Beat egg whites and ¼ tsp. cream of tartar till whites hold shape. Fold egg whites into ricotta mixture and pour into a pie shell; see index for pie shell recipe. Bake at 350° for 40 to 45 minutes. Let cool and then refrigerate.

Recipe Note: Total recipe is 56 carbohydrates and 111 protein. Includes crust.

NO BAKE PEANUT BUTTER PIE

1 baked nut pie crust (see index)
1 8 oz. package cream cheese,
  softened
1 c. splenda
1 tsp. vanilla extract

⅔ c. unsweetened peanut butter
1 tsp. liquid sweetener Sweet &
  Low
½ cup whipping cream
¼ tsp. cream of tartar

Beat cream cheese, splenda and vanilla together. Stir in peanut butter. Set aside. In another bowl mix whipping cream with liquid sweetener and cream of tartar and beat till it holds its shape. Fold the whipped cream into the peanut butter mixture. Pour into a nut pie crust. See index for crust recipe.

Recipe Note: Total recipe 94 carbohydrates and 32 protein. Includes pie crust.

PEANUT BUTTER PIE

Baking
Low Carb

1 unbaked pie crust (see index)
4 eggs
½ c. water
¾ c. whipping cream
¾ c. splenda
1 tbl. liquid sweetener Sweet &
  Low

1 tsp. molasses
⅓ c. unsweetened peanut butter
1 tsp. vanilla extract
2 tsp. maple extract
½ tsp. xanthan gum
½ c. chopped peanuts

Beat eggs, water, whipping cream, splenda, sweetener, molasses, peanut butter, vanilla, maple and gum. Pour into pie crust. See index for pie crust recipe. Sprinkle nuts over the top. Bake at 350° for 30 - 40 min. until set and lightly brown. Chill before serving and keep refrigerated.

Recipe Note: Total recipe 79 carbohydrates and 97 protein. This includes pie crust.

PUMPKIN PIE

1 unbaked pie shell (see index)
1 15 ounce can Pumpkin
2 eggs
½ c. splenda
2 tsp. liquid sweetener Sweet &
  Low

1 tsp. cinnamon
½ tsp. ginger
1 c. whipping cream

Beat eggs; add splenda, sweetener, cinnamon, ginger. Stir in pumpkin and whipping cream till smooth. Pour into a pie plate sprayed with Pam or a pie shell. See index for a nut pie crust recipe, if you wish to put in a crust. Bake at 350° for 35 to 45 min., until set.

Recipe Note: Total carbohydrate 52 and 11 protein. Does not include pie shell.

290631-99

RHUBARB CUSTARD PIE

I unbaked pie crust (see index)
4 eggs
½ c. water
I c. whipping cream
½ c. splenda
I tbl. liquid sweetener Sweet &
  Low

¼ c. melted butter
2 tsp. vanilla
½ tsp. grated orange peel
½ tsp. xanthan gum
2½ c. finely cut rhubarb
½ c. splenda

Combine rhubarb and ½ c. splenda and microwave for 1 min to softened. Beat eggs, water, whipping cream, splenda, sweetener, butter, vanilla, orange peel and gum. Stir in rhubarb. Pour into pie crust. See index for pie crust recipe. Bake 350° for 35 - 45 minutes until set and lightly brown. Chill before serving and keep refrigerated.

Recipe Note: Total recipe 74 carbohydrates and 78 protein. This includes pie crust.

Pastry

COCONUT CRUST

¼ c. butter melted
2 c. unsweetened coconut

3 tbl. splenda

Combine butter, splenda and coconut. Press evenly into a 8 or 9 inch pie pan. Bake in slow 300° oven for 20 to 35 minutes till golden brown. Cool.

Recipe Note: Whole crust is 26 carbohydrates and 4 protein.

NUT PIE CRUST

I c. fine ground nuts
2 tbl. splenda
3 to 4 tbl. melted butter

I tbl. oat flour
¼ tsp. cinnamon

Combine nuts, splenda, melted butter, oat flour and cinnamon; mix. Press into the bottom of a 9 inch pie plate. Bake at 350° for 5 to 10 min. Watch carefully so it doesn't burn. Cool before adding filling.

Recipe Note: Carbohydrates 40 and 8 protein.

PIE CRUST

**Baking
Low Carb**

¾ c. vanilla whey protein powder
⅓ c. oat flour
2 tbl. finely ground almonds

½ c. shortening
1 to 2 tbl. cold water

Mix together vanilla whey protein powder, oat flour, and almonds. Cut shortening into flour mixture with two knives or a pastry blender, using a cutting motion. It will resemble peas when done. Add water 1 tbl at a time till dough hold together. Refrigerate till chilled for easier handling. This dough can be rolled out by putting between two pieces of wax paper or you can put the dough in a 9" pie plate and pat it up the sides to the rim. Spray Pam on pie tin before putting crust in it. Oil your hands to make it easier to manage dough if using patting method. If you take the pie crust over the rim, be sure to put alum foil around edges to prevent it browning to much, before pie filling is done. Pour filling into crust and bake. If you need a completely baked crust, pierce crust with a fork and bake at 350° for 5 to 10 min. Watch so it doesn't burn.

Recipe Note: Whole crust has 30 carbohydrates and 71 protein.

Flavored Crusts

2 tsp. lemon peel
1 tsp. orange peel
2 tbl. baking cocoa
2 tsp. cinnamon

¼ c. ground nuts
¼ tsp. nutmeg
1 tsp. instant coffee to water

To add flavor to the regular pie crust recipe add one of the above.

6

290631-99

Desserts

My Favorite Recipe

_____
_____
_____
_____
_____
_____
_____
_____
_____
_____
_____
_____
_____
_____
_____
_____
_____
_____
_____

Desserts

CANNOLI FILLING

1 15 oz. container of Ricotta
⅓ c. splenda
1 tsp. cinnamon
1 tsp. vanilla

1 tsp. liquid sweetener Sweet &
Low
½ tsp. orange peel
2 tbl. heavy whipping cream

Combine ricotta, splenda, cinnamon, vanilla, splenda, sweetener, orange peel, and heavy whipping cream; mix till blended. Refrigerate until ready to serve. Spoon into crepes and gently roll them up. See index for crepe recipe. 6 servings.

Recipe Note: 5 carbohydrate and 5 protein each.

CHOCOLATE CAKE ROLL

1½ c. vanilla whey protein powder
¼ c. oat flour
2 tsp. baking powder
¼ c. baking cocoa
⅓ c. splenda

2 egg
¾ c. oil
¼ c. heavy whipping cream
½ c. water
2 tsp. vanilla extract

Combine vanilla whey protein, oat flour, baking powder, baking cocoa and splenda. Mix egg, oil, water, and heavy whipping cream and vanilla together and then combine with dry ingredient. Beat 2 minutes. Use a 10 x 15 inch cookie sheet with sides or a jelly roll pan. Line pan with waxed paper, aluminum foil or cooking parchment paper; generously grease foil or waxed paper with shortening. Spread batter in prepared pan and bake at 350° for 10 to 15 minutes. Check with toothpick. Immediately loosen cake from edges of pan and turn upside down onto a dish towel. Carefully remove paper. While hot, carefully roll cake and towel from narrow end. Cool on wire rack at least 30 minutes till cool. Unroll cake and remove towel. Frost with frosting or whip cream. Slice into 10 pieces.

Recipe Note: Each slice of cake is 3 carbohydrates and 14 protein.

CHOCOLATE COVERED STRAWBERRIES

**Baking
Low Carb**

1 pint of LARGE strawberries
5 tbl. butter
½ c. baking cocoa
¼ c. splenda

1 tsp. liquid Sweet & Low
1 tsp. vanilla extract
⅓ c. heavy whipping cream

Wash strawberries and drain on towel till dry. Melt butter and stir in cocoa. Add liquid sweetener, splenda and vanilla. Stir in cream till you have smooth sauce. Dip each strawberries in to top of green stem. Refrigerate. Usually about 20 to 25 strawberries.

Recipe Note: Total recipe carbohydrates 55 and 5 protein.

CHOCOLATE FLUFF

⅔ c. heavy whip cream
2 tsp. baking cocoa
⅓ c. vanilla whey protein powder

1 tbl. splenda
½ tsp. almond extract

Stir together whip cream, baking cocoa, vanilla whey protein, splenda and almond extract. Mix slowly till most of the lumps are gone; whip till mixture holds it fluffy and holds it shape. Put in two small dessert bowls; refrigerate.

Recipe Note: 4.5 carbohydrate and 6 protein each.

CUSTARD SAUCE

1 c. whipping cream
1 c. water
4 egg yolks
1 tsp. vanilla

⅓ c. splenda
¼ tsp. liquid sweetener Sweet & Low

Combine whip cream and water in a saucepan and scald the mixture. Beat egg yolks till they are thick and pale. Slowly pour the scalded mixture into the yolk mixture, stirring constantly. Pour the combined mixture back in the saucepan and cook over a low heat, stirring constantly until it is thick enough to coat the back of the spoon. Add vanilla, splenda and sweetener and stir till blended. Refrigerate.

Recipe Note: Total recipe has 16 carbohydrates and 2 protein.

290631-99

DESSERT CREPES

2 eggs
¼ c. water
¼ c. heavy cream
½ tsp. vanilla

1 tbl. oil
1 tsp. splenda
½ c. vanilla whey protein powder
1 tbl. oat four

With a mixer combine eggs, water, heavy cream, vanilla, oil, splenda, oat flour and whey protein till blended. Preheat a 8 inch skillet. Keep flame low. Put 1 tsp. of oil in the bottom and spoon in 3 tablespoons of the batter. Swirl the pan till crepe covers the bottom evenly. Small bubbles will form...doesn't take long to cook...pick up pan and if batter doesn't move you can carefully flip the crepe and cook for another 10 seconds or so. Put on plate to cool. Place wax paper between crepes. Makes 6 crepes. Keep in refrigerator till ready to use. Serve with strawberries or serve warm with your favorite sugar free syrup.

Recipe Note: Each crepe has 1.5 carbohydrate and 9 protein.

DESSERT GELATIN

1 pkg. any flavor sugar free Jello
1 c. boiling water
1 c. heavy whip cream

⅓ c. vanilla whey protein powder
2 tbl. splenda

Combine Jello and boiling water and then cool till syrupy. In a bowl combine Jello mixture, whipping cream, vanilla whey and splenda and beat at high speed till fluffy....about 5 minutes. Pour into small bowls and refrigerate. 4 servings.

Recipe Note: 2 Carbohydrate and 8 protein each.

EASY CHEESECAKE

½ cup whipping cream
2 tbl. Splenda
8 oz. cream cheese
½ c. sour cream

1 tsp. vanilla
1 tsp. liquid sweetener Sweet &
Low

Beat whipping cream with splenda till holds its shape. Mix cream cheese, sweetener, vanilla and sour cream till smooth. Stir whipping cream and cream cheese mixture together. Pour into pie plate and re-frigerate.

Recipe Note: Total recipe 17 carbohydrates and 10 protein.

EGG NOG CHEESECAKE

1¼ c. heavy whipping cream
1 4 oz. carton egg beaters
1 c. splenda
1 tsp. vanilla or rum extract

¼ tsp. nutmeg
⅛ tsp. cinnamon
1 tsp. xanthan gum
8 oz. pkg. of cream cheese

In a sauce pan, over a low heat, combine whipping cream, egg beater, splenda, vanilla, nutmeg and cinnamon. Blend with whisk and stir continually till warm and steamy (not boiling). Whisk in xanthan gum. Add cream cheese and stir till melted in to mixture. Pour into a 9 inch pie dish and refrigerate. See index for a nut pie crust recipe, if you wish to put in a crust.

Recipe Note: Total recipe 42 carbohydrates and 15 protein. Does not include crust.

HOME MADE ICE CREAM BARS

1-1 qt. ice cream maker
2½ c. heavy whipping cream
½ c. water
⅓ c. vanilla whey protein
⅓ c. splenda

2 tsp. liquid sweetener Sweet &
Low
2 tsp. caramel extract
2 tsp. coffee extract

Combine whipping cream, water, vanilla whey protein, splenda, liquid sweetener, and extracts ; mix well. Pour into ice cream maker and prepare according to ice cream makers directions for soft serve. Drop by large spoonfuls on wax paper lined cookie sheets to make 10 mounds and put a stick in each one. Freeze.

Recipe Note: Each bar 2.5 carbohydrate and 4 protein.

KOOL-AID FLUFF

⅔ c. heavy whipping cream
⅓ c. vanilla whey protein

1 tbl. splenda
¼ tsp. any flavor Kool aid mix

In a bowl, add Kool-Aid to whipping cream. Stir in vanilla whey protein and splenda. Beat on high till fluffy. Put into two small bowls and refrigerate.

Recipe Note: Each serving 1.5 carbohydrate and 5 protein.

290631-99

LEMON CHEESECAKE

1 small box Lemon sugar free Jello
1 c. boiling water
15 oz. container Ricotta cheese

8 oz. cream cheese
1½ tsp. lemon extract
½ c. splenda

Stir Jello into hot water; refrigerate until Jello is syrupy. Blend together ricotta cheese, cream cheese, splenda and extract at medium speed until smooth. Add Jello to mixture; mix and pour into 9" pie plate. See index for a nut pie crust recipe, if you wish to put in a crust. Chill till set.

Recipe Note: Total cheesecake is 36 carbohydrates and 34 protein. Does not include crust.

PISTACHIO CHEESE DELIGHT

1 pkg. Pistachio instant sugar free
   pudding
1 pkg. Knox unflavored gelatin
⅔ c. water
⅓ c. heavy cream

⅓ c. water
8 oz. pkg. cream cheese softened
½ tsp. liquid sweetener Sweet &
   Low

In a deep measuring cup or bowl, sprinkle 2 pkgs. of gelatin over ⅔ cup of water and stir; let stand 2 min. Microwave 40 seconds, stir and let stand while you prepare pudding. With mixer, mix pudding, ⅓ c. water and ⅓ c. heavy whip cream. Add cream cheese and sweetener; blend well and then add gelatin mixture and continue blending. Pour into a 9 inch glass pie pan and refrigerate. See index for a nut pie crust recipe, if you wish to put in a crust. Serve with whipping cream

Recipe Note: Total recipe 34 carbohydrates and 7 protein. Does not include crust.

PUMPKIN CAKE ROLL

1½ c. vanilla whey protein powder
¼ c. oat flour
2 tsp. baking powder
1 tsp. baking soda
⅓ c. splenda
1 tsp. cinnamon
½ tsp. nutmeg

2 egg
¾ c. oil
1 tsp. liquid sweetener Sweet & Low
⅓ c. pumpkin
⅓ c. water

Combine vanilla whey protein, oat flour, baking powder, cinnamon, nutmeg, and splenda. Mix egg, oil, sweetener, water, and pumpkin together and then mix with dry ingredient. Beat 2 minutes. Use a 10 x 15 cookie sheet with sides or a jelly roll pan. Line pan with waxed paper, aluminum foil or cooking parchment paper; generously grease foil or waxed paper with shortening. Spread batter in prepared pan, tap pan on counter to settle bubbles, and bake at 350° for 10 to 15 minutes. Check with toothpick. Immediately loosen cake from edges of pan and turn upside down onto a dish towel. carefully remove paper. While hot, carefully roll cake and towel up. cool on wire rack at least 30 minutes till cool. Unroll cake and remove towel. Trim edges if too crisp. Frost with filling. Slice.

Recipe Note: With filling: whole cake 60 Carbohydrates and 142 Protein.

Filling

½ c. splenda
1 tbl. liquid sweetener Sweet & Low

1 8 oz. pkg. cream cheese
4 tbl butter
½ tsp. vanilla

Cream all the ingredient together and spread on cooled cake. Roll and chill.

PUMPKIN CHEESECAKE

16 oz. cream cheese
3 eggs
⅔ c. splenda
1 tsp. vanilla

1 c. canned pumpkin
1 tsp. cinnamon
2 tsp. liquid sweetener Sweet & Low

Beat cream cheese and add eggs, splenda and vanilla. Remove 1 cup of the cream cheese mixture and combine it with the canned pumpkin, cinnamon and sweetener. Alternating, layer pumpkin and cream cheese batters in a 9 inch Pam sprayed pie pan. Cut through batters with a knife to create a marbled effect. Bake at 400° for 40 to 50 min or until cheesecake springs back slightly when touched. See index for a nut pie crust recipe, if you wish to put in a crust. Serves 12.

Recipe Note: Total recipe 62 carbohydrates and 45 protein. Does not include crust.

290631-99

QUICK CHEESE PIE

16 oz. cream cheese
3 eggs

1 tsp. vanilla
²/₃ c. splenda

Desserts

Beat cream cheese and add eggs, splenda and vanilla. When well blended, pour into Pam sprayed 9" pie pan. See index for a nut pie crust recipe, if you wish to put in a crust. Bake 350° for 30 min. Remove and cool for 20 min.

Topping

1 c. sour cream
3 tbls. splenda

1 tsp. vanilla

Stir together sour cream, splenda and vanilla. Pour on top of pie and bake 10 min more. Chill and serve.

Recipe Note: Total recipe 48 carbohydrates 36 protein. Does not include crust.

RHUBARB CRISP

4 c. fresh diced rhubarb
²/₃ c. Splenda
³/₄ tsp. cinnamon

1 c. vanilla whey protein powder
¼ c. chopped walnuts
⅓ c. butter

Take ⅓ cup of splenda and mix it together with the rhubarb. Microwave 3 to 5 minutes to softened. At this point if you like your rhubarb sweeter, you could add some liquid sweetener. Grease 8 inch pan and put the warm rhubarb in this pan. Combine other ⅓ cup of splenda, cinnamon, nuts and vanilla whey protein powder and cut into the butter to make a crumbly topping. Put topping on rhubarb and bake at 375° for 10 to 12 minutes. Makes 6 servings.

Recipe Note: Each serving is 8 carbohydrates and 15 protein.

SHORTCAKE

**Baking
Low Carb**

½ c. vanilla whey protein
¼ c. high gluten flour
¼ c. oat flour
2 tsp. baking powder

¼ tsp. baking soda
¼ c. shortening
¼ c. heavy whipping cream
2 tbl. water

Mix together vanilla whey protein, gluten flour, oat flour, baking powder and baking soda; cut into shortening. Mix cream and water and stir into shortening mixture. Drop by large tablespoon on to cookie sheet. Bake at 375° 8 min. till lightly brown on top and bottom. Cut in half and fill with strawberries and top with whip cream.

Recipe Note: Each biscuit 4.3 carbohydrate and 10 protein.

Recipe Favorites

290631-99

Breads & Muffins

My Favorite Recipe

_____
_____
_____
_____
_____
_____
_____
_____
_____
_____
_____
_____
_____
_____
_____
_____
_____
_____
_____
_____
_____

Breads & Muffins

Breads

ANISE MUFFINS

⅔ c. oil
½ c. water
⅓ c. heavy whipping cream
3 eggs
1 tsp. anise extract
2 tsp. liquid sweetener Sweet &
  Low

2 tbl. splenda
2 tsp. orange peel
1¼ c. vanilla whey protein powder
2 tbl. oat flour
2 tbl. high gluten flour
2 tsp. baking powder
¼ c. chopped almonds

Combine oil, water, whipping cream, eggs, anise and liquid sweetener; mix. Add splenda, orange peel, vanilla whey protein powder, oat flour, gluten flour and baking powder; mix till moistened. Stir in nuts. Pour into 12 greased muffin tins. Bake at 350° for 10 to 15 min. Keep an eye on them so the don't over cook.

Recipe Note: Each muffin has 4 carbohydrates and 11 protein.

ANISE ZUCCHINI BREAD

2 c. shredded, unpeeled zucchini
2 eggs
½ c. oil
⅓ c. heavy whipping cream
¼ c. water
1½ tsp. anise extract

⅓ c. splenda
½ c. chopped almonds
1½ c. vanilla whey protein powder
3 tbl. high gluten flour
⅓ c. oat flour
2 tsp. baking powder

Combine zucchini, eggs, oil, cream, anise extract and water; Add splenda, almonds, gluten flour, whey protein powder, oat flour and baking powder; mix till moistened. Pour into greased bread pan. Bake 40 to 45 min at 350°.

Recipe Note: Total loaf is 78 carbohydrates and 163 protein.

BACON MUFFINS

⅔ c. oil
½ c. water
⅓ c. heavy whipping cream
3 eggs
1 tsp. vanilla

1¼ c. vanilla whey protein powder
2 tbl. oat flour
2 tbl. high gluten flour
2 tsp. baking powder
6 slices fried bacon

Combine oil, water, whipping cream, vanilla and eggs; mix. Add vanilla whey protein powder, oat flour, gluten flour and baking powder; mix till moistened. Break bacon into small pieces and stir into batter. Pour into 12 greased muffin tins. Bake at 350° for 10 to 15 min. Keep an eye on them so they don't over cook.

Recipe Note: Each muffin 3 carbohydrates and 11 protein.

BANANA BREAD

1 8" very ripe banana
2 eggs
½ c. oil
⅓ heavy whipping cream
⅔ c. water
⅓ c. splenda
2 tsp. banana extract
1½ c. vanilla whey protein powder

¼ c. oat flour
3 tbl. high gluten flour
2 tsp. baking powder
¼ tsp. baking soda
1½ tsp. cinnamon
¼ tsp. nutmeg
¼ cup chopped walnuts

Using a fork, mash banana till fairly smooth. Combine eggs, oil, whip cream, water, banana, splenda and, extract; mix. Add whey protein powder, gluten flour, oat flour, baking powder, soda, cinnamon, nutmeg and chopped walnuts. Stir till moistened. Pour into greased bread pan. Bake at 350° for 40 to 45 min. Do not over bake.

Recipe Note: Total loaf: Carbohydrates 90 carbohydrates 163 protein.

290631-99

BANANA MUFFINS

⅔ c. oil
½ c. water
⅓ c. heavy whipping cream
2 eggs
1 8" very ripe banana
2 tsp. banana extract

2 tbl Splenda
1¼ c. vanilla whey protein powder
2 tbl oat flour
2 tbl high gluten flour
2 tsp. baking powder
¼ cup chopped walnuts

Using a fork, mash banana till fairly smooth. Mix oil, water, whipping cream and eggs till blended. Add banana and extract and mix. Mix in Splenda, whey, oat flour, gluten and baking powder and mix till moistened. Stir in nuts. Pour into 12 greased muffin tins. Bake at 350° for 10 to 15 minutes....keep an eye on them so they don't over cook.

Recipe Note: Each muffin has 4 carbohydrates and 11 protein.

BREAD

1 Bread Machine
½ c. water
½ c. heavy whip cream
1 tbl. oil
1 egg
¼ tsp. salt

1 c. high gluten flour
¼ c. psyllium fiber
½ c. oat flour
½ c. vanilla whey protein powder
1 pkg. Rapid rise yeast

To your bread machine add the ingredients in the order that follows. Add water, cream, oil, egg, slightly mixed, salt, gluten flour, oat flour, vanilla whey protein powder, and yeast. Set your bread machine according to directions for Rapid Bake (2 hours).

Recipe Note: 60 carbohydrates and 98 protein for loaf.

CHOCOLATE MUFFINS

**Baking
Low Carb**

⅔ c. oil
½ c. water
⅓ c. heavy whipping cream
3 eggs
I tsp. vanilla
I tbl. liquid sweetener Sweet &
  Low
2 tbl. splenda

I c. vanilla whey protein powder
2 tbl. oat flour
2 tbl. high gluten flour
2 tsp. baking powder
¼ c. baking cocoa
2 tsp. orange peel
¼ c. chopped walnuts

Combine oil, water, whipping cream, eggs, vanilla and liquid sweetener; mix. Add splenda, vanilla whey protein powder, oat flour, gluten flour, baking powder, orange peel and baking cocoa; mix till moistened. Stir in nuts. Pour into 12 greased muffin tins. Bake at 350° for 10 to 15 min. Keep an eye on them so they don't over cook.

Recipe Note: Each muffin has 3 carbohydrates and 11 protein.

CHOCOLATE ZUCCHINI BREAD

2 c. shredded, unpeeled zucchini
2 eggs
½ c. oil
⅓ c. whipping cream
¼ c. water
⅓ c. splenda
I tbl. liquid sweetener Sweet &
  Low

I tsp. almond extract
⅓ c. baking cocoa
I¼ c. vanilla whey protein powder
3 tbl. high gluten flour
¼ c. oat flour
2 tsp. baking powder

Combine zucchini, eggs, oil, cream, splenda, sweetener, almond extract, and water; mix. Add baking cocoa, vanilla whey protein, high gluten flour, oat flour and baking powder; mix till moistened. Pour into greased bread pan. Bake 40 to 45 min. at 350°.

Recipe Note: Total loaf is 78 carbohydrates and 163 protein.

290631-99

COCOA NUT COFFEE CAKE

2/3 c. oil
1 c. sour cream
1/2 c. water
3 eggs
2 tsp. orange extract
1 1/4 c. vanilla whey protein powder
1/4 c. oat flour
2 tbl. high gluten flour

1/4 cup baking cocoa
1 tsp. baking soda
1 tbl. baking powder
1/2 c. Splenda
1 tbl. liquid sweetener Sweet & Low
1 tbl. grated orange peel

Combine sour cream, oil, water and eggs, orange extract; mix. Add whey powder, oat flour, gluten flour, cocoa, baking soda, baking powder, cinnamon, orange peel, liquid sweetener, Splenda and mix till blended. Pour into a Spring form pan.

Topping:

1/2 c. chopped nuts
1 tbl. baking cocoa

1/4 tsp. cinnamon
1/4 c. Splenda

Combine nuts, cocoa, cinnamon and splenda and sprinkle over the top of the coffee cake. Bake 350° for 30 to 35 min. Cut into 12 pieces.

Recipe Note: 6 carbohydrates and 11 protein per slice.

COCONUT COFFEE CAKE

2 eggs
1/2 c. oil
1/2 c. water
1 tsp. vanilla
1 c. vanilla whey protein powder

2 tbl high gluten flour
1/4 c. oat flour
1/3 c. splenda
1/4 c. unsweetened coconut

Combine eggs, oil, water and extract; mix. Add whey powder, gluten flour, oat flour, coconut and splenda and mix till moistened. Pour into greased 8 inch cake pan.

Topping

2 tbl. unsweetened coconut
1 tbl. Splenda

1/4 tsp. cinnamon

Combine eggs, oil, water and extract; mix. Add whey powder, gluten flour, oat flour, cinnamon, coconut and splenda and mix till moistened. Pour into greased 8 inch pan. Bake 15 minutes at 375°.

Recipe Note: 8 slices at 5 carbohydrates and 11 protein each.

EASY COFFEE CAKE

**Baking
Low Carb**

4 large eggs
⅛ c. water
¼ c. heavy cream
3 tbl. oil
¾ cup vanilla whey protein
  powder

1 tbl. baking powder
1 tsp. cinnamon
2 tbl Splenda

Combine eggs, water, heavy cream, oil; mix. Add Whey powder, baking powder and cinnamon and mix till moistened. Pour into a greased 8" cake pan.

Topping:

¼ cup ground nuts
½ tsp. molasses

1 tbl vanilla whey protein powder
2 tbl cold butter

For topping, combine nuts, molasses, whey powder and cut into the cold butter to make a crumbly topping... Sprinkle on top and bake 15 min at 375°.

Recipe Note: 8 slices at 4 carbohydrates and 12 protein each.

FRUIT CREAM CHEESE SPREAD

2 tbls. mashed strawberries or
  raspberries
8 ounces cream cheese room
  temperature

2 tbl. splenda

Whip the cream cheese and splenda together. Stir in berries and serve with your favorite bread or muffin.

Recipe Note: Each tablespoon 1 carbohydrate and 1 protein.

20

LEMON BREAD

1 c. sauerkraut
2 eggs
½ c. oil
1 tsp. vanilla
⅓ c. heavy whipping cream
¼ c. water
1 tsp. liquid sweetener Sweet &
  Low
1 tsp. lemon extract

⅓ c. splenda
½ c. walnuts
1½ c. vanilla whey protein powder
⅓ c. high gluten flour
⅓ c. oat flour
2 tsp. baking powder
1 tbl. lemon peel
2 tsp. orange peel
1 tsp. cinnamon

Thoroughly rinse sauerkraut; drain. Combine sauerkraut, eggs, oil, vanilla, cream, water, liquid sweetener and extract; mix. Add splenda, walnuts, gluten flour, whey powder, oat flour, baking powder, lemon peel and cinnamon; mix till moistened. Pour into a greased bread pan. Bake 40 to 45 min. at 350°.

Recipe Note: Total loaf is 78 carbohydrates and 163 protein.

LEMON PECAN COFFEE CAKE

½ cup oil
⅓ cup water
2 eggs
3 tbl lemon juice
½ tsp. almond extract
2 tbl. liquid sweetener Sweet and
  Low

¾ c. Splenda
1 c. vanilla whey protein powder
¼ c. oat flour
2 tbl. high gluten flour
1 tbl baking powder
1 tsp. baking soda
¼ cup chopped pecans

Combine oil, water, eggs, lemon juice and almond extract; mix. Add sweet and low, splenda, whey powder, oat flour, baking powder, baking soda and gluten flour (no nuts); mix till moistened. Pour into greased 8 inch cake pan. Sprinkle with chopped pecans. Bake 15 minutes at 375°. Cut into 8 pieces.

Recipe Note: 5 carbohydrates and 14 protein.

LEMON POPPY SEED MUFFINS

Baking
Low Carb

3 eggs
3 tbl. oil
¼ c. heavy whipping cream
¾ cup vanilla whey protein
   powder
2 tsp. baking powder

⅓ c. Splenda
¼ tsp. cinnamon
¼ c. chopped walnuts
1 tbl. poppy seeds
1 tbl. grated lemon peel
½ tsp. grated orange peel

Mix eggs, oil, and cream together. Add whey powder, baking powder, splenda, cinnamon, walnuts, poppy seeds, lemon peel and orange peel. Mix till moistened. Pour into 9 sprayed muffin tins. Bake 375° for 8 min.

Recipe Note: 3.5 carbohydrates and 9 protein per muffin.

NUT MUFFINS

⅔ c. oil
½ c. water
⅓ c. heavy whipping cream
3 eggs
1 tsp. vanilla
2 tsp. liquid sweetener Sweet &
   Low

2 tbl. splenda
1¼ c. vanilla whey protein powder
2 tbl. oat flour
2 tbl. high gluten flour
2 tsp. baking powder
½ c. fine ground pecans

Combine oil, water, whipping cream, eggs, vanilla and liquid sweetener; mix. Add splenda, vanilla whey protein powder, oat flour, gluten flour and baking powder; mix till moistened. Stir in nuts. Pour into 12 greased muffin tins. Bake at 350° for 10 to 15 min. Keep an eye on them so they don't over cook.

Recipe Note: Each muffin has 3 carbohydrates and 11 protein.

290631-99

ORANGE MUFFINS

2/3 c. oil
1/2 c. water
1/4 tsp. unsweetened orange Kool
aid drink mix
1/3 c. heavy whipping cream
3 eggs
2 tsp. liquid sweetener Sweet &
Low

2 tbl. splenda
1 1/4 c. vanilla whey protein powder
2 tbl. oat flour
2 tbl. high gluten flour
2 tsp. baking powder
1 tsp. orange peel
1/4 c. chopped walnuts

Mix Kool aid in water. Combine oil, orange water, whipping cream, eggs, and liquid sweetener. Add splenda, vanilla whey protein powder, oat flour, gluten flour, orange peel and baking powder; mix till moistened. Stir in nuts. Pour into 12 greased muffin tins. Bake at 350° for 10 to 15 min. Keep on eye on them so they don't over cook.

Recipe Note: Each muffin has 3 carbohydrates and 11 protein.

ORANGE ZUCCHINI NUT BREAD

2 c. shredded unpeeled zucchini
2 eggs
1/2 c. oil
1/3 c. heavy whipping cream
1/4 c. water
1/4 tsp. unsweetened Orange Kool
aid drink mix
1/3 c. Splenda

1 tbl. liquid sweetener Sweet &
Low
1 1/2 c. vanilla whey protein powder
3 tbl. high gluten flour
1/3 c. oat flour
2 tsp. baking powder
1 tbl. orange peel
1/2 c. chopped walnuts

Mix Kool Aid mix in 1/4 c. water. Combine zucchini, eggs, oil, cream and orange water; mix. Add splenda, liquid sweetener, whey protein powder, gluten flour, oat flour, orange peel and baking powder; mix till moistened. Pour into greased bread pan. Bake 40 to 45 min. at 350°.

Recipe Note: Total loaf is 78 carbohydrates and 163 protein.

PEANUT BUTTER MUFFINS

Baking
Low Carb

⅓ c. oil
½ c. water
⅓ c. heavy whipping cream
½ c. unsweetened peanut butter
3 eggs
1 tsp. vanilla
1 tbl. liquid sweetener Sweet &
Low

2 tbl. splenda
1¼ c. vanilla whey protein powder
2 tbl. oat flour
2 tbl. high gluten flour
2 tsp. baking powder

Combine oil, water, whipping cream, eggs, peanut butter and liquid sweetener; mix. Add splenda, vanilla whey protein, oat flour, gluten flour and baking powder; mix till moistened. Pour into 12 greased muffin tins. Bake 350° for 10 to 15 min. Keep an eye on them so they don't over cook.

Recipe Note: Each muffin has 4 carbohydrates and 12 protein.

PEANUT BUTTER ZUCCHINI BREAD

2 c. shredded unpeeled zucchini
2 eggs
¼ c. oil
⅔ c. unsweetened peanut butter
⅓ c. heavy whipping cream
¼ c. water
1 tbl. liquid sweetener Sweet &
Low

⅓ c. splenda
1½ c. vanilla whey protein powder
3 tbl. high gluten flour
¼ c. oat flour
2 tsp. baking powder

Combine zucchini, eggs, oil, peanut butter, cream, water, and liquid sweetener; mix. Add splenda, vanilla whey protein, gluten flour, oat flour, baking powder; mix till moistened. Pour into greased bread pan. Bake 40 to 45 min. at 350°.

Recipe Note: Total loaf is 98 carbohydrates and 190 protein.

290631-99

PISTACHIO COFFEE CAKE

2 eggs
½ c. oil
½ c. water
2 tsp. Pistachio Extract
1 c. vanilla whey protein powder
2 Tbl. high gluten flour

1 Tbl. baking powder
¼ c. oat flour
½ tsp. salt
⅓ c. Splenda
2 tbl. Chopped Pistachio's

Combine eggs, oil, water and extract; mix. Add whey powder, gluten flour, oat flour, baking powder, salt, and Splenda (no nuts) and mix till blended. Pour into a greased 8-inch cake pan. Sprinkle with nuts. Bake at 375° for 12 to 15 minutes. Cut into 8 pieces.

Recipe Note: 5 carbohydrates and 14 protein each piece.

POPPY SEED COFFEE CAKE

3 eggs
½ c. water
⅔ c. oil
1 c. sour cream
2 tsp. lemon extract
1¼ c. vanilla whey protein powder
¼ c. oat flour
2 tbl. high gluten flour

1 tsp. baking soda
1 tbl. baking powder
1 tsp. cinnamon
2 tbl. poppy seed
1 tbl. lemon peel
1 tbl orange peel
1 c. Splenda

Combine eggs, water, oil, sour cream, lemon extract; mix. Add whey powder, oat flour, gluten flour, baking soda, baking powder, cinnamon, splenda, poppy seed, lemon peel, and orange peel; mix till blended. Pour into a greased spring form pan. Bake 350° for 30 to 35 minutes. Cut into 12 pieces.

Recipe Note: 5 carbohydrates and 11 protein.

POPPY SEED ZUCCHINI BREAD

Baking
Low Carb

2 c. shredded unpeeled zucchini
2 eggs
½ c. oil
⅓ c. heavy whipping cream
¼ c. water
¼ tsp. unsweetened Lemon aid
  Kool aid drink mix
⅓ c. splenda

1 tbl. liquid sweetener Sweet &
  Low
1½ c. vanilla whey protein
3 tbl. high gluten flour
⅓ c. oat flour
2 tsp. baking powder
2 tbl. Poppy seeds

Mix Kool aid mix in ¼ c. water. Combine zucchini, eggs, oil, cream and lemon water; mix. Add splenda, liquid sweetener, whey protein powder, gluten flour, oat flour, poppy seeds and baking powder; mix till moistened. Pour into greased bread pan. Bake 40 to 45 min at 350°.

Recipe Note: Total loaf is 66 carbohydrates and 114 protein.

PUMPKIN BREAD

½ c. oil
1 c. canned pumpkin
2 eggs
⅓ c. heavy whipping cream
¼ c. water
⅓ c. Splenda
½ c. chopped walnuts
1½ c. vanilla whey protein powder

3 tbl. high gluten flour
⅓ c. oat flour
2 tsp. baking powder
1 tsp. baking soda
1 tsp. salt
3 tsp. cinnamon
1 tsp. nutmeg

Combine oil, eggs, pumpkin, whipping cream and water; mix. Add Splenda, walnuts, whey powder, gluten flour, oat flour, baking powder, baking soda, salt, cinnamon and nutmeg. Pour into greased bread pan. Bake at 350° for 40 to 45 min. Do not over bake.

Recipe Note: Total loaf is 76 carbohydrates and 116 protein.

290631-99

PUMPKIN MUFFINS

²/₃ c. oil
½ c. water
⅓ c. heavy whipping cream
2 eggs
⅓ c. canned pumpkin
2 tsp. liquid sweetener Sweet &
 Low
3 tbl. Splenda

1¼ c. vanilla whey protein powder
2 tbl. oat flour
2 tbl. high gluten flour
2 tsp. baking powder
½ tsp. nutmeg
1 tsp. cinnamon
¼ c. chopped nuts

Combine oil, water, whipping cream, eggs, pumpkin and liquid sweetener; mix. Add splenda, vanilla whey protein, oat flour, high gluten flour, baking powder, nutmeg and cinnamon; mix till moistened. Stir in nuts. Pour into 12 greased muffin tins. Bake at 350° for 10 to 15 min. Keep an eye on them so the don't over bake.

Recipe Note: Each muffin has 4 carbohydrates and 11 protein.

RHUBARB BREAD

1½ c. diced rhubarb
2 eggs
½ c. oil
⅓ c. heavy whipping cream
¼ c. water
⅓ c. Splenda
1 tsp. molasses
1½ c. vanilla whey protein powder

3 tbl. high gluten flour
⅓ c. oat flour
2 tsp. baking powder
1 tsp. baking soda
1 tsp. salt
2 tsp. cinnamon
½ cup chopped nuts

Combine rhubarb, eggs, oil, cream, water, Splenda and molasses; mix. Add whey protein powder, gluten flour, oat flour, baking powder, baking soda, salt, cinnamon, nuts and mix till moistened. Pour into greased bread pan and bake at 350° for 40 to 45 min. Do not over bake.

Recipe Note: Total loaf is 83 carbohydrates and 117 protein.

SOUR CREAM COFFEE CAKE

**Baking
Low Carb**

I cup sour cream
⅔ c. oil
½ c. water
3 eggs
2 tsp. almond extract
1¼ c. vanilla whey protein powder
¼ c. oat flour

2 tbl. High Gluten Flour
I tsp. baking soda
I tbl. baking powder
2 tsp. cinnamon
½ c. Splenda
I tbl. liquid sweetener Sweet &
Low

Combine sour cream, oil, water and eggs, almond; mix. Add whey powder, oat flour, gluten flour, baking soda, baking powder, cinnamon, sweetener, Splenda and mix till blended. Pour into a greased Spring form pan.

Topping

½ c. chopped nuts
2 T. Splenda

¼ tsp. cinnamon

Combine nuts, 2 T. Splenda and cinnamon and sprinkle over top of coffee cake. Bake 350° for 30 to 35 minutes. Cut into 12 pieces.

Recipe Note: 6 carbohydrate and II protein per slice.

SWEET ZUCCHINI BREAD

2 c. shredded, un peeled zucchini
2 eggs
½ c. oil
⅓ c. heavy whipping cream
¼ c. water
⅓ c. Splenda

½ c. chopped walnuts
1½ c. vanilla whey protein powder
3 tbl. high gluten flour
⅓ c. oat flour
2 tsp. baking powder
3 tsp. cinnamon

Combine zucchini, eggs, oil, cream and water; mix. Add splenda, walnuts, gluten flour, whey powder, oat flour, baking powder, baking soda, salt and cinnamon; mix till moistened. Pour into greased bread pan. Bake 40 to 45 min at 350°.

Recipe Note: Total loaf is 78 carbohydrates and II8 protein.

290631-99

Cakes & Toppings

My Favorite Recipe

_____
_____
_____
_____
_____
_____
_____
_____
_____
_____
_____
_____
_____
_____
_____
_____
_____
_____
_____
_____
_____

Cakes & Toppings

Cakes

¾ c. shortening
¾ c. Splenda
4 eggs.
1 tsp. lemon extract
2 tsp. lemon peel
1 tsp. liquid sweetener Sweet &
Low

2 c. vanilla whey protein powder
½ c. oat flour
2 tbl. high gluten flour
1 tbl. baking powder
1 tsp. baking soda
¾ c. water
½ c. heavy whipping cream

Cream shortening and splenda. Add eggs one at a time and beat after each. Mix in extract and lemon peel and liquid sweetener. Add vanilla whey protein, oat flour, gluten flour, baking powder, and baking soda; mix. Pour into greased 9 x 13 pan and bake at 350° for 15 to 20 minutes. Test with toothpicks. Do not over bake.

Recipe Note: Cut into 18 pieces. Each 4 carbohydrates and 9 protein.

ALMOND SNACK CAKE

1 c. vanilla whey protein powder
¼ c. oat flour
1 tbl. baking powder
⅓ c. splenda
1 egg

¾ c. oil
¼ c. water
¼. c. heavy whipping cream
2 tsp. almond extract
¼ c. slivered almond

Before you begin the cake you may want to add flavor to the almonds by toasting in the microwave with 1 tbl butter for 1 min. Drain on a paper towel. Combine vanilla whey protein powder, oat flour, baking powder and splenda in a bowl. Mix egg, oil, water, extract and whipping cream in a bowl and stir in dry ingredient. Pour into a greased 8 inch baking pan and tap on the counter a few times to settle bubbles. Bake 350° for 15 to 20 min. Test with toothpick, do not over bake or will be dry.

Recipe Note: 12 serving have 3 carbohydrates and 3 protein each serving.

BROWNIES

**Baking
Low Carb**

5 tbls. butter
¼ c. baking cocoa
2 eggs
¼ c. heavy cream
¼ c. water
1 tsp. vanilla
¼ cup Splenda

1 tsp. liquid sweetener Sweet & Low
¾ cup vanilla whey protein powder
2 tbl. oat flour
1 tbl. baking powder
3 tbl. chopped walnuts

Melt butter and stir in cocoa. Add to eggs, water, heavy cream, vanilla, splenda, and sweetener; mix. Add Whey protein, oat flour and baking powder and mix till moistened. Pour into greased 8 inch pan. Sprinkle nuts on top and bake at 375° for 15 minutes. Cut into 16 pieces.

Recipe Note: Each square 1.4 carbohydrate and 5 protein.

BUTTER CAKE

¾ c. softened butter
¾ c. splenda
4 eggs
1 tsp. vanilla extract
1 tsp. liquid sweetener Sweet & Low

2 c. vanilla whey protein powder
½ c. oat flour
2 tbl. high gluten flour
1 tbl. baking powder
¾ c. water
½ c. heavy whipping cream

Cream butter and splenda. Add eggs one at a time and beat after each. Mix in extract and liquid sweetener. In a bowl combine whey powder, oat flour, gluten flour and baking powder. Mix together cream and water and alternating with flour mixture add to batter; mix well. Pour into 9 x 13 pan and bake at 350° for 15 to 20 minutes. Test with toothpick...do not over bake. While still hot prick the entire cake with a fork and pour Butter sauce over the top.

Recipe Note: Cut into 18 pieces. Each 5.5 carbohydrate and 13 protein.

Butter Sauce

1 c. splenda
¼ c. water

½ c. butter
1 tbl. vanilla

Heat altogether until butter is melted...do not boil.

290631-99

BUTTER FROSTING

½ c. warm. water
½ c. vanilla whey protein powder
1 tsp. vanilla extract

¾ c. butter (room temperature
⅓ c. splenda

Combine warm water and vanilla whey protein powder and stir until whey dissolves. Add extract. Beat butter and splenda together. Add whey mixture and beat until smooth and spreadable. If after beating, the mixture is too thin or separated, add additional whey protein one tablespoon at a time, beating after each addition. Don't let it get too thick. Frost 9 x 12 inch cake.

Recipe Note: Total recipe 12 carbohydrates and 23 protein.

Chocolate Frosting

3 tbls. baking cocoa
2 tsp. liquid sweetener Sweet &
  Low

Add to Butter frosting.

Lemon Butter Frosting

1 tsp. lemon peel
1 tsp. lemon extract

1 tsp. liquid sweetener Sweet &
  Low

Add to butter frosting recipe and eliminate vanilla extract.

Orange Frosting

½ tsp. orange peel
1 tsp. orange extract

1 tsp. liquid sweetener Sweet &
  Low

Add to butter recipe and eliminate vanilla extract.

Coffee Butter Frosting

2 tsp. coffee extract
1 tsp. liquid sweetener Sweet &
  Low

Add to butter frosting recipe and eliminate vanilla extract.

Caramel Frosting

1 tsp. molasses

Add to butter frosting recipe.

BUTTER GLAZES

1 stick of butter (room
 temperature)
¼ cup splenda

1 tsp. extract
¼ c. heavy whipping cream

Mix splenda and whipping cream together till splenda dissolves. Beat with butter and extract till smooth. Vary extracts for different flavors. Spread on a warm cake for a glaze or serve with coffee cake or muffins as a spread.

Recipe Note: Total carbohydrates 8 and 0 protein.

CHOCOLATE CAKE

1 c. shortening
¾ c. Splenda
4 eggs
2 tsp. liquid sweetener Sweet &
 Low
1 tsp. vanilla extract
¼ baking cocoa
1¾ c. vanilla whey protein
 powder

½ c. oat flour
2 tbl. high gluten flour
1 tbl. baking powder
1 tsp. baking soda
¾ c. water
½ c. heavy whipping cream

Cream shortening and splenda. Add eggs one at a time and beat after each. Mix in extract and sweetener. In a bowl combine baking cocoa, whey powder, oat flour, high gluten flour, baking powder, and baking soda. Mix together cream and water and alternating with flour mixture add to batter; mix well. Pour into greased 9 x 13 pan and bake at 350° for 15 to 20 minutes. Test with toothpick. Do not over bake.

Recipe Note: Cut into 18 pieces. Each 4 carbohydrates and 13 Protein.

290631-99

CHOCOLATE ZUCCHINI SNACK CAKE

3/4 c. vanilla whey protein
1/4 c. oat flour
1 tbl. baking powder
1/4 c. baking cocoa
1 tsp. cinnamon
1/3 c. splenda

1 egg
1/2 c. oil
1/2 c. grated zucchini
2 tbl. heavy whipping cream
1/4 c. water

Combine vanilla whey protein, oat flour, baking powder, cocoa. cinnamon and splenda. Mix egg, oil, zucchini, heavy whipping cream and water and then stir in dry ingredients. Pour into a greased 8 inch baking pan and tap on counter a few times to settle bubbles. Bake 350° for 15 to 20 min. Test with toothpick, do not over bake or it will be dry.

Recipe Note: 12 servings 3 carbohydrates and 3 protein each serving.

COFFEE BARS

1/4 c. oil
2 eggs
1/4 c. heavy cream
1/4 c. hot water
1 tsp. instant coffee
1/4 c. splenda
1 tsp. liquid sweetener Sweet &
  Low

3/4 c. vanilla whey protein powder
2 tbl. oat flour
1 tbl. baking powder
2 tsp. cinnamon
1/4 c. mini chocolate chips

Dissolve coffee in water. Mix oil, eggs, heavy cream, water, splenda and sweetener together. Add whey protein, oat flour, baking powder and cinnamon and mix till moistened. Pour into 8 inch pan. Tap on counter to settle bubbles and sprinkle chocolate chips on top. Bake at 375° for 12 to 15 min. Do not over bake.

Recipe Note: Cut into 16 pieces 3 carbohydrate and 4 protein.

290631-99

CREAM CHEESE BROWNIES

Baking Low Carb

5 tbls. butter
¼ c. baking cocoa
2 eggs
¼ c. heavy cream
¼ c. water
¼ c. splenda

1 tsp. liquid sweetener Sweet & Low
¾ c. vanilla whey protein powder
2 tbl. oat flour
1 tbl. baking powder

Melt butter and stir in cocoa. Add to eggs, water, heavy cream, vanilla, splenda, and sweetener; mix. Add whey protein, oat flour, and baking powder and mix till moistened. Pour into greased 8 inch pan.

Cream Cheese Filling

3 to 4 oz. cream cheese
3 tbl. butter
3 tbl. Splenda

1 egg
2 tbl. vanilla whey protein
½ tsp. vanilla

Mix cream cheese, butter, splenda, egg, vanilla whey protein and vanilla together and spoon over the top the brownie batter. Bake 350° for 15 minutes. Cut into 16 pieces.

Recipe Note: Each piece 2.5 carbohydrate and 5 protein.

CREAM CHEESE FROSTING

4 oz. pkg. of cream cheese (room temperature)
2 tbls. butter (softened)
½ c. Splenda

½ tsp. liquid sweetener saccharin
¼ c. heavy whipping cream
1 tsp. almond

Mix splenda, extract and whipping cream together till Splenda dissolves. Beat with butter and cream cheese till fluffy. Frosts 8 inch cake. For additional flavors check the Butter Frosting recipe and follow instructions.

Recipe Note: Total recipe 16 carbohydrates and 6 protein.

290631-99

GINGERBREAD SNACK CAKE

1 c. vanilla whey protein powder
¼ c. oat flour
2 tsp. baking powder
1 tsp. baking soda
1 tsp. cinnamon
1 tsp. ginger
½ tsp. liquid sweetener Sweet &
  Low

2 tsp. molasses
1 egg
¾ c. oil
¼ c. water
¼ c. heavy whipping cream

Combine vanilla whey protein, oat flour, baking powder, baking soda, cinnamon and ginger in a bowl. Mix egg, oil, water, molasses, and whipping cream in bowl and then stir in dry ingredients. Pour into a greased 8 inch baking pan and tap on a counter a few times to settle bubbles. Bake 350° for 15 to 20 min. Test with toothpick, do not over bake or it will be dry.

Recipe Note: 12 servings 3 carbohydrates and 2 protein. Serve with whipped cream.

LEMON CAKE

¾ c. shortening
¾ cup Splenda
4 eggs
1 tsp. lemon extract
2 tsp. lemon peel
1 tsp. liquid sweetener Sweet &
  Low

2 c. vanilla whey protein powder
½ c. oat flour
2 tbl high gluten flour
1 tbl. baking powder
1 tsp. baking soda
¾ c. water
½ c. heavy whipping cream

Cream shortening and splenda. Add eggs one at a time and beat after each. Mix in extract, lemon peel and liquid sweetener. In a bowl combine whey powder, oat flour, high gluten flour, baking powder and baking soda. Mix together cream and water and alternating with flour mixture add to batter; mix well. Pour into a greased 9 x 13 pan. Bake at 350° 18 to 20 minutes. Do not over bake. Check with toothpick. Cut into 16 servings.

Recipe Note: 4 carbohydrates and 12 protein for each piece.

LICORICE CAKE

¾ c. shortening
¾ c. splenda
4 eggs
1 tsp. orange extract
1½ tsp. anise extract
1 tbl. orange peel
1 tsp. liquid sweetener Sweet & Low

2 c. vanilla whey protein powder
½ c. oat flour
2 tbl. high gluten flour
1 tbl. baking powder
1 tsp. baking soda
¾ c. water
½ c. heavy whipping cream

Cream shortening and splenda. Add eggs one at a time and beat after each. Add orange extract, anise extract, orange peel and liquid sweetener; mix. In a bowl combine whey powder, oat flour, high gluten flour, baking powder and baking soda. Mix together cream and water and alternating with flour mixture, add to batter; mix well. Pour into 9 x 13 pan. Bake at 350° for 18 to 20 minutes. Do not over bake. Check with toothpick. Cut into 16 servings.

Recipe Note: 4 carbohydrates and 12 protein for each piece.

MOCHA SNACK CAKE

1 c. vanilla whey protein powder
¼ c. oat flour
1 tbl. baking powder
⅓ c. splenda
2 tbl. baking cocoa
½ tsp. liquid sweetener Sweet & Low

1 egg
¾ c. oil
¼ c. water
¼ c. heavy whipping cream
2 tsp. coffee extract
¼ c. almonds

Combine vanilla whey protein, oat flour, baking powder, cocoa and splenda in a bowl. Mix liquid sweetener, egg, oil, water, extract and whipping cream in a bowl and then stir in dry ingredients. Pour into a 8 inch baking pan and tap the counter a few times to settle bubbles. Sprinkle almonds on the top. Bake 350° for 15 to 20 min. Test with toothpick, do not over bake or it will be dry.

Recipe Note: 12 servings. 4 carbohydrates and 3 protein per serving.

290631-99

ORANGE BROWNIES

5 tbls. butter
¼ c. baking cocoa
2 eggs
¼ c. heavy cream
¼ c. water
1 tsp. orange extract
1 tsp. vanilla extract
¼ c. Splenda

1 tsp. liquid sweetener Sweet & Low
¾ c. vanilla whey protein powder
2 tbl. oat flour
2 tsp. baking powder
1 tsp. baking soda
1 tsp. orange peel

Melt butter and stir in cocoa. Add to eggs, water, heavy cream, extracts, splenda, and sweetener; mix. Add whey protein, oat flour, baking powder, baking soda and orange peel; mix till moistened. Pour into a greased 8 inch pan. Bake at 375° for 15 minutes. While still hot butter with glaze. Cut into 16 pieces.

Recipe Note: Each square 1.5 carbohydrate and 5 protein.

Orange Glaze

½ stick butter softened
2 tbl. splenda

1 tsp. orange extract

Mix together butter, splenda and lemon extract. Spread on warm brownies.

ORANGE ZUCCHINI SNACK CAKE

1 c. vanilla whey protein powder
¼ c. oat flour
2 tsp. baking powder
1 tsp. baking soda
⅓ c. splenda
½ tsp. nutmeg
1 tsp. cinnamon

1½ tsp. orange peel
1 egg
½ c. oil
½ c. grated zucchini
2 tbl. heavy whipping cream
¼ c. water

Combine vanilla whey protein, oat flour, baking powder, baking soda, nutmeg, cinnamon, orange peel and splenda in a bowl. Mix egg, oil, water, zucchini, cream and water in a bowl and then stir in dry ingredient. Pour into a greased 8 inch baking pan and tap on the counter a few times to settle bubbles. Bake 350° for 15 to 20 min. Test with toothpick, do not over bake or will be dry.

Recipe Note: 12 servings 3 carbohydrates and 3 protein each.

Lemon Glaze

½ stick butter room temperature
2 tbl. splenda

1 tsp. lemon extract

Mix together butter, splenda and lemon extract together. Butter the cake while it's hot.

PEANUT BUTTER BROWNIES

**Baking
Low Carb**

5 tbls. butter
¼ c. baking cocoa
2 eggs
¼ c. heavy cream
¼ c. water
1 tsp. vanilla

¼ c. Splenda
1 tsp. liquid sweetener Sweet &
 Low
¾ c. vanilla whey protein powder
2 tbl. oat flour
1 tbl. baking powder

Melt butter and stir in cocoa. Add to eggs, water, heavy cream, vanilla, splenda, and sweetener; mix. Add Whey Protein, oat flour and baking powder and mix till moistened. Pour into greased 8 inch pan.

Peanut Butter Topping

¼ cup natural peanut butter
3 tbl. butter
2 tbl. Splenda

1 Egg
2 tbl. Vanilla whey protein
 powder

Mix all ingredients together and spoon on top of brownie batter. Bake at 350° for 15 minutes. Cut into 16 pieces.

Recipe Note: 2.5 Carbohydrates and 5 protein.

PEANUT BUTTER CUP SNACK CAKE

1 c. vanilla whey protein powder
¼ c. oat flour
1 tbl. baking powder
⅓ c. splenda
1 egg

¼ c. unsweetened peanut butter
¾ c. oil
¼ c. water
¼ c. heavy whipping cream
¼ c. mini chocolate chips

Combine vanilla whey protein powder, oat flour, baking powder and splenda in a bowl. Mix egg, peanut butter, oil, water, and heavy whipping cream in a bowl and then stir in dry ingredients. Pour into a greased 8 inch baking pan and tap on the counter a few times to settle bubbles. Sprinkle chocolate chips. Bake 350° for 15 to 20 min. Test with toothpick, do not over bake or will be dry.

Recipe Note: 12 servings 5 carbohydrates and 3 protein each serving.

290631-99

PUMPKIN SNACK CAKE

1 c. vanilla whey protein
¼ c. oat flour
2 tsp. baking powder
1 tsp. baking soda
½ tsp. nutmeg
1 tsp. cinnamon

⅓ c. splenda
1 egg
½ c. oil
¼ c. pumpkin
2 tbl heavy whipping cream
¼ c. water

Combine vanilla whey protein, oat flour, baking powder, baking soda, nutmeg, cinnamon and splenda in a bowl. Mix egg, oil, water, pumpkin, whipping cream and water and then stir in dry ingredients. Pour into 8 inch baking pan and tap on a counter a few times to settle bubbles. Bake at 350° for 15 to 20 min. Test with a toothpick, do not over bake or it will be dry.

Recipe Note: 12 servings 3 carbohydrates and 3 protein per serving. Good with whipped cream.

SAUERKRAUT LEMON SNACK CAKE

1 c. vanilla whey protein powder
¼ c. oat flour
2 tsp. baking powder
⅓ c. Splenda
1½ tsp. lemon peel
½ tsp. orange peel
½ tsp. liquid sweetener Sweet &
  Low

1 tsp. lemon extract
½ c. sauerkraut
1 egg
½ c. oil
¼ c. water

Rinse sauerkraut thoroughly; drain. Combine vanilla whey protein powder, oat flour, baking powder, baking soda, and splenda in a bowl. Mix lemon peel, orange peel, liquid sweetener, extract, egg, oil, water and sauerkraut in a bowl and then stir in dry ingredients. Pour into a greased 8 inch baking pan and tap on counter a few times to settle bubbles. Bake 350° for 15 to 20 min. Test with toothpick, do not over bake or will be dry.

Recipe Note: 12 servings 3 carbohydrates and 3 protein each serving.

SOUR CREAM SNACK CAKE

1 c. vanilla whey protein powder
¼ c. oat flour
2 tsp. baking powder
1 tsp. baking soda
⅓ c. splenda
2 tsp. cinnamon

1 egg
½ c. oil
¼ c. water
½ c. sour cream
¼ c. chopped walnuts

Combine vanilla whey protein powder, oat flour, baking powder, baking soda, splenda and cinnamon in a bowl. Mix egg, oil, water and sour cream in a bowl and then stir in dry ingredients. Pour into a greased 8 inch baking pan and tap on a counter a few times to settle bubbles. Sprinkle nuts on top. Bake 350° for 15 to 20 min. Test with toothpick, do not over bake or it will be dry.

Recipe Note: 12 servings 3 carbs. and 3 protein each.

STRAWBERRY MOUSSE MERINGUE CUPS

4 egg whites
½ tsp. cream of tartar

½ c. splenda

Beat 4 egg whites till they become frothy; beat in cream of tartar. Slowly add splenda while continuing to beat. Beat until stiff peaks form. On baking sheet lined with parchment paper, spoon mixture into 8 mounds. Make an indentation in each one so they look like cups. Bake at 250° for 1½ hours until they are light brown and dry. Turn off oven and leave till oven cools off. Set aside and prepare strawberry mousse.

Strawberry Filling

1 pkg. (20 oz.) frozen strawberries
2 tbl. splenda
¼ tsp. liquid sweetener Sweet &
 Low

1 tsp. xanthan gum
1 cup whip cream
1 tbl. splenda

Thaw strawberries and coarsely chop them. Stir in 2 tbl. splenda, xanthan gum and ¼ tsp. sweetener. In a saucepan bring mixture to a boil and stir till it thickens. Refrigerate till cooled. In a bowl beat the whip cream and tbl.. splenda till stiff peaks form. Stir one half of whipping cream in to cooled strawberry mixture. Fold in the remaining whip cream and spoon into meringues and serve.

Recipe Note: Makes 8 servings at 3 carbohydrates each.

290631-99

STRAWBERRY SNACK CAKE

1 c. vanilla whey protein powder
1/4 c. oat flour
2 tsp. baking powder
1 tsp. baking soda
1/3 c. splenda
1/2 tsp. liquid sweetener Sweet &
  low

1 package of Wyler's Strawberry
  drink (makes 2 qts.)
1 egg
3/4 c. oil
1/4 c. water
1/4 c. heavy whipping cream

Combine vanilla whey protein, oat flour, baking powder, baking soda, strawberry mix and splenda. Mix egg, oil, water, sweetener, and whipping cream and then stir in dry ingredients. Pour into a greased 8 inch. baking pan and tap on a counter a few times to settle bubbles. Bake at 350° for 15 to 20 min. Test with a toothpick, do not over bake or it will be dry.

Recipe Note: 12 servings 3 carbohydrates and 3 protein per serving. Slice in half and put whipped cream inside and a few fresh strawberries. Top with more whip cream. Be sure to add extra carbs. for whip cream and strawberries.

YELLOW CAKE

3/4 c. shortening
3/4 c. Splenda
4 eggs
1 tsp. vanilla extract
1 tsp. liquid sweetener Sweet &
  Low

2 c. vanilla whey protein powder
1/2 c. oat flour
2 tbl. high gluten flour
1 tbl. baking powder
3/4 c. water
1/2 c. heavy whipping cream

Cream shortening and splenda. Add eggs one at a time and beat after each. Mix in extract and liquid sweetener. In a bowl combine whey powder, oat flour, gluten flour and baking powder. Mix together cream and water and alternating with flour mixture add to batter; mix well Pour into 9 x 13 pan and bake at 350° for 15 to 20 minutes. Test with toothpick...do not over bake.

Recipe Note: Cut into 18 pieces. Each 4 carbohydrates and 12 protein.

Baking
Low Carb

Cookies

My Favorite Recipe

_____
_____
_____
_____
_____
_____
_____
_____
_____
_____
_____
_____
_____
_____
_____
_____
_____
_____
_____
_____
_____

Cookies

BUTTERSCOTCH CHIP COOKIES

2 sticks butter room temperature
½ c. shortening
⅓ c. splenda
1 tsp. molasses
1 egg

1 c. vanilla whey protein powder
½ c. oat flour
1 tsp. baking powder
1 tsp. baking soda
½ c. butterscotch baking chips

Cream softened butter, shortening, molasses and splenda; add egg and mix. Add vanilla whey protein powder, oat flour, baking powder and baking soda; mix till blended. Stir in butterscotch chips. Drop by tsp. on cookie sheet and bake at 350° for 5 to 6 min. Watch so they don't burn as you are using butter. Makes approximately 5 dozen cookies.

Recipe Note: 2 carbohydrate and 1.5 protein each.

CHOCOLATE CHIP COOKIES

2 sticks butter room temperature
½ c. shortening
⅓ c. splenda
1 tsp. molasses
1 egg
1 c. vanilla whey protein powder

½ c. oat flour
1 tsp. baking powder
1 tsp. baking soda
½ c. mini chocolate chips
¼ c. chopped walnuts

Cream softened butter, shortening, molasses and splenda; add egg and mix. Add vanilla whey protein, oat flour, baking powder and baking soda. Stir in chocolate chips and walnuts. Drop by tsp. on cookie sheet and bake at 350° for 5 to 6 min. Watch so they don't burn as you are using butter. Makes approximately 5 dozen cookies.

Recipe Note: 2 Carbohydrates and 1.5 protein each.

CHOCOLATE CHOCOLATE CHIP COOKIES

**Baking
Low Carb**

2 sticks butter room temperature
½ c. shortening
⅓ c. splenda
1 tsp. molasses
1 egg
1 c. vanilla whey protein powder

½ c. oat flour
1 tsp, baking powder
1 tsp. baking soda
¼ c. baking cocoa
½ c. mini chocolate chips

Cream softened butter, shortening, molasses and splenda; add egg and mix. Add vanilla whey protein, oat flour, baking powder, baking soda, and baking cocoa; mix till blended. Stir in chocolate chips. Drop by tsp. on cookie sheet and bake at 350° for 5 to 6 min. Watch so they don't burn as you are using butter. Makes approximately 5 dozen cookies.

Recipe Note: 2 carbohydrates and 1.5 protein each.

CHOCOLATE COCONUT CHEWS

2 sticks butter room temperature
½ c. shortening
⅔ c. splenda
1 egg
1 tsp. almond extract

1 c. vanilla whey protein powder
½ c. + 2 tbls. oat flour
¼ c. baking cocoa
1 tsp. baking powder
½ c. unsweetened coconut

Cream softened butter, shortening and splenda; add egg and mix. Add vanilla whey protein, oat flour, baking cocoa, and baking powder. Stir in coconut. Bake at 350° for 5 to 7 min. Watch so they don't burn as you are using butter. Makes approximately 5 dozen cookies.

Recipe Note: 1 carbohydrate and 1.5 protein.

290631-99

CHOCOLATE COOKIE BARS

1 c. heavy whipping cream
2 egg yolks
¼ c. baking cocoa
1 tsp. liquid sweetener Sweet &
  Low

½ c. splenda
1 tsp. vanilla

Combine whipping cream, egg yolks, baking cocoa, splenda and sweetener and 1 tsp. vanilla. Whisk and cook over low heat until it thickens. Set aside to cool.

Crust

1¾ c. vanilla whey protein
⅓ c. splenda
¼ c. baking cocoa

2 sticks butter
½ c. ground nuts
¼ c. mini chocolate chips

Combine whey protein, splenda and baking cocoa. Cut in 2 sticks of butter till crumbly mixture. Press firmly on to the bottom of a 13 x 9 inch baking pan. Bake at 350 ° for 10 min to 15 min to set. Over the top of the cooked crust pour the whipping cream mixture you prepared. Top with the ground nuts and chocolate chips and bake for 15 to 20 minutes more to set. Makes 36 bars.

Recipe Note: 3 carbohydrates and 5 protein each.

CHOCOLATE PEANUT BUTTER CHIP COOKIES

2 sticks butter room temperature
½ c. shortening
⅓ c. splenda
1 egg
1 c. vanilla whey protein powder

½ c. oat flour
1 tsp. baking powder
¼ c. baking cocoa
½ c. peanut butter baking chips

Cream softened butter, shortening, and splenda; add egg and mix. Add vanilla whey protein powder, oat flour, baking powder and cocoa and mix till blended. Drop by tsp. on cookie sheet. Place 3 peanut butter chips on each cookie and bake at 350° for 5 to 6 min. Watch so they don't burn as you are using butter. Makes approximately 5 dozen cookies.

Recipe Note: 2 carbohydrates and 1.5 protein each.

CHOCOLATE SANDWICH COOKIES

Baking
Low Carb

2 sticks butter room temperature
½ c. shortening
⅓ c. splenda
1 tsp. molasses
1 egg

1 c. vanilla whey protein powder
½ c. oat flour
1 tsp. baking powder
1 tsp. baking soda
¼ c. baking cocoa

Cream softened butter, shortening, molasses, and splenda; add egg and mix. Add vanilla whey protein, oat flour, baking powder, baking soda, and baking cocoa; mix till blended. Drop by tsp. on cookie sheet and bake at 350° for 5 to 7 min. Cool and frost one cookie and put other on top. Makes about 2½ dozen cookies frosted.

Recipe Note: About 3 carbs. per cookies with filling and 3.5 protein.

Cookie filling

½ c. warm water
½ c. vanilla whey protein powder
1 tsp. vanilla extract
¾ c. butter room temperature

⅓ c. splenda
2 tsp. liquid sweetener Sweet & Low

Combine warm water and vanilla whey protein and stir until whey dissolves. Add extract. Beat butter, splenda, and liquid sweetener together. Add whey mixture and beat until smooth and spreadable. If after beating, the mixture is too thin or separated, add additional whey protein one tablespoon at a time, beating after each addition. Don't let get too thick.

CHOCOLATE THUMBPRINT COOKIE

2 sticks butter room temperature
½ c. shortening
⅔ c. splenda
1 egg
1 c. vanilla whey protein powder

½ c. oat flour
¼ c. baking cocoa
1 tsp. baking powder
½ c. ground nuts

Cream butter, shortening, and splenda; add egg and mix. Add vanilla whey, oat flour, baking cocoa and baking powder and mix till blended. Refrigerate for ½ hour (Make jelly recipe while waiting for dough to chill). Put ground nuts in small bowl. Roll dough into small balls and roll lightly in nuts. Press a finger in each one to make indentation; add ½ tsp. jelly. Bake at 350° for 5 to 7 min. Watch so they don't burn as you are using butter. Makes approximately 5 dozen. cookies

Recipe Note: 3 carbohydrates and 2 protein each.

Jelly

2 c. of fresh or frozen Raspberries
  or Strawberries

5 tbl. splenda
2 tsp. xanthan gum

Place in food processor and blend all ingredients.

290631-99

CHRISTMAS COOKIES

2 sticks butter room temperature
½ c. shortening
⅓ c. splenda
l egg
¾ tsp. of pkg. of Wyler's 2 qt.
  drink in Cherry or Strawberry

l c. vanilla whey protein powder
½ c. oat flour
l tsp. baking powder
⅓ c. splenda

Cream softened butter, shortening and splenda; add egg and mix. Add Wyler's drink mix, vanilla whey protein powder, oat flour and baking powder and mix till blended. Refrigerate ½ hr. Put ⅓ c. splenda in small bowl and roll dough in to small balls; roll lightly in splenda. Bake at 350° for 5 to 7 minutes...watch so they don't burn. Approximately 5 dozen. Make another batch using lime flavor drink for Christmas colors.

Recipe Note: l carbohydrate and 2 protein each.

CINNAMON COOKIES

2 sticks butter room temperature
½ c. shortening
⅔ c. splenda
l egg

l c. vanilla whey protein powder
½ c. oat flour
l tsp. baking powder
2 tsp. cinnamon

Cream softened butter, shortening and splenda; add egg and mix. Add vanilla whey protein, oat flour, baking powder and cinnamon; mix till blended. Bake at 350° for 5 to 7 min. Watch so they don't burn as you are using butter. Makes approximately 5 dozen cookies.

Recipe Note: l carbohydrate and 2 protein each.

CINNAMON PECAN COOKIES

2 sticks butter (room
  temperature)
½ c. shortening
⅔ c. splenda
l egg

l c. vanilla whey protein powder
½ c. oat flour
l tsp. baking powder
l tsp. cinnamon
½ c. chopped pecans

Cream softened butter, shortening and splenda; add egg and mix. Add dry ingredients and mix till blended. Drop by tsp. on cookie sheet and bake at 350° for 5 to 6 min. Watch so they don't burn as you are using butter. Makes approximately 5 dozen cookies

Recipe Note: l carbohydrate and 2 protein each.

COFFEE DROP COOKIES

2 sticks butter (room
  temperature)
½ c. shortening
⅔ c. splenda
1 tsp. molasses
1 egg

2 tsp. coffee extract
1 tsp. cinnamon
1 c. vanilla whey protein powder
½ c. & 2 tbl oat flour
1 tsp. baking powder
½ tsp. baking soda

Cream softened butter, shortening, molasses and splenda; add egg and mix. Add dry ingredients and mix till blended. Drop by tsp. on cookie sheet and bake at 350° for 5 to 6 min. Watch so they don't burn as you are using butter. Makes approximately 5 dozen cookies

Recipe Note: 1 carbohydrate and 2 protein each.

CRISSCROSS PEANUT BUTTER

½ c. unsweetened peanut butter
¼ c. shortening
¼ c. butter
1 tsp. molasses
½ c. splenda

1 egg
½ c. oat flour
½ c. vanilla whey protein powder
2 tsp. baking powder

Cream peanut butter, shortening and butter; add splenda and eggs; mix. Add oat flour, vanilla whey protein, and baking powder and mix till blended. Make into ¾" ball and flatten with fork dipped in vanilla whey to prevent sticking. Bake at 350° 6 to 7 min and watch so they don't burn as you are using butter. Makes approximately 3 dozen.

Recipe Note: 3 carbohydrates and 2.5 protein each.

DOUBLE CHOCOLATE MINT COOKIES

2 sticks butter room temperature
½ c. shortening
⅓ c. splenda
1 egg
1 tsp. mint extract

1 c. vanilla whey protein powder
½ c. oat flour
1 tsp. baking powder
¼ c. baking cocoa
½ c. mini chocolate chips

Cream butter, shortening and splenda. Add egg and extract; mix. Add vanilla whey protein, oat flour, baking powder and baking cocoa; mix till blended. Stir in chocolate chips. Drop by tsp. on cookie sheet and bake at 350° for 6 - 7 min. Watch so they don't burn as you are using butter. Makes approximately 5 dozen cookies.

Recipe Note: 2.3 carbohydrates and 1.5 protein each.

290631-99

GINGER COOKIES

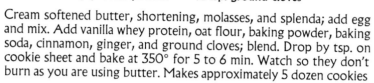

2 sticks butter room temperature	½ c. oat flour
½ c. shortening	1 tsp. baking powder
⅔ c. splenda	½ tsp. baking soda
1 tsp. molasses	1 tsp. cinnamon
1 egg	1 tsp. ginger
1 c. vanilla whey protein powder	½ tsp. ground cloves

Cream softened butter, shortening, molasses, and splenda; add egg and mix. Add vanilla whey protein, oat flour, baking powder, baking soda, cinnamon, ginger, and ground cloves; blend. Drop by tsp. on cookie sheet and bake at 350° for 5 to 6 min. Watch so they don't burn as you are using butter. Makes approximately 5 dozen cookies

Recipe Note: 1 carbohydrate and 2 protein each.

LEMON DROPS

2 sticks butter room temperature	1 tsp. lemon peel
½ c. shortening	1 c. vanilla whey protein powder
⅔ c. splenda	½ c. oat flour
1 egg	1 tsp. baking powder
1 tsp. lemon extract	½ tsp. baking soda

Cream softened butter, shortening and splenda. Add egg, extract; mix. Blend in lemon peel, vanilla whey protein, oat flour, baking powder and baking soda. Drop by tsp. on cookie sheet. Bake 350° for 5 to 6 min. Watch so they don't burn. Makes approximately 4 dozen cookies.

Recipe Note: 1 carbohydrate and 2 protein.

M & M COOKIES

2 sticks butter room temperature	1 c. vanilla whey protein powder
½ c. shortening	½ c. oat flour
⅓ c. splenda	1 tsp. baking powder
1 tsp. molasses	1 tsp. baking soda
1 egg	½ c. mini M & M's baking bits

Cream softened butter, shortening, molasses and splenda; add egg and mix. Add vanilla whey protein, oat flour, baking powder, and soda and mix till blended. Stir in M & M chocolate chips. Drop by tsp. on cookie sheet and bake at 350° for 5 to 6 min. Watch so they don't burn as you are using butter. Makes approximately 5 dozen cookies.

Recipe Note: 2 carbohydrates and 1.5 protein each.

MACADAMIA TEA COOKIES

1 c. butter room temperature
½ c. shortening
⅔ c. splenda
1 egg

1 c. vanilla whey protein powder
½ c. oat flour
1 tsp. baking powder
¾ c. chopped macadamia nuts

Cream softened butter, shortening and splenda; add egg and mix. Add vanilla whey protein, oat flour, and 1 tsp. baking powder and mix till blended; add nuts. Drop by tsp. on cookie sheet and bake at 350° for 5 to 6 min. Watch so they don't burn as you are using butter. Makes approximately 5 dozen cookies.

Recipe Note: 1 carbohydrate and 2 protein each.

MERINGUE COOKIES

3 egg whites
¼ tsp. cream of tartar

⅓ c. splenda
1 tbl. lemon peel

Beat egg whites and cream of tartar on high until soft peaks form. Beat in Splenda a little at a time and continue beating till stiff peaks form. Gentle fold in lemon peel. Drop by tablespoonfuls on Pam sprayed cookie sheets. Bake at 250° for about 1 hour. Turn oven off and leave cookies in oven till it cools off. Makes about 20. Store in tightly closed container.

Recipe Note: Less than 1 carb. and protein per cookie.

MOCK DATE COOKIE BARS

1 c. fine ground pecans
2 tbl. splenda

3 tbl. melted butter
1 tbl. oat flour

To make a crust, mix pecans, splenda and oat flour; add melted butter. Press into the bottom of of a 8 inch cake pan. Bake at 350° for 5 min.

Top Layer

3 eggs
3 tbl. water
¾ c. splenda
1 tsp. molasses

2 tbl oat flour
¼ tsp. baking soda
¼ tsp. baking powder

Combine eggs, water, molasses and splenda. Add oat flour, baking soda and baking powder; mix. Pour on top of baked crust and bake at 350° for 15 minutes. Cut into 16 bars.

Recipe Note: 4 carbohydrates and 4.5 protein each.

290631-99

MOLASSES COOKIES

2 sticks butter room temperature
½ c. shortening
1 tbl. molasses
⅓ c. splenda
1 egg
1 c. vanilla whey protein powder

½ c. oat flour
1 tsp. baking powder
½ tsp. baking soda
½ tsp. cinnamon
1 tsp. ginger

Cookies

Cream softened butter, shortening and splenda; add egg and mix. Add vanilla whey protein, oat flour, baking powder, baking soda, cinnamon and ginger and mix till blended. Drop by tsp. on cookie sheet and bake at 350° for 5 to 6 min. Watch so they don't burn as you are using butter. Makes approximately 5 dozen cookies

Recipe Note: 1 carbohydrate and 2 protein each.

NUTMEG COOKIES

2 sticks butter room temperature
½ c. shortening
⅓ c. splenda
1 egg
1 c. vanilla whey protein powder

½ c. oat flour
1 tsp. baking powder
⅛ tsp. nutmeg
⅓ c. splenda
⅓ tsp. nutmeg

Cream softened butter, shortening and splenda; add egg and mix. Add vanilla whey protein, oat flour, baking powder and ⅛ tsp. nutmeg; mix till blended. Refrigerate for ½ hour. Put ⅓ c. splenda and ⅛ tsp. nutmeg in small bowl. Roll dough into small balls and roll lightly in sugar mixture. Bake at 350° for 5 to 7 minutes...watch so they don't burn. Makes approximately 5 dozen cookies.

Recipe Note: 1 carbohydrate and 2 protein each.

ORANGE COCONUT DROPS

1 c. butter room temperature
½ c. shortening
⅔ c. splenda
1 egg
1 tsp. orange peel

1 tsp. orange extract
1 c. vanilla whey protein powder
½ c. oat flour
1 tsp. baking powder
½ c. unsweetened coconut

Cream softened butter, shortening and splenda; add egg and mix. Add rind, extract, vanilla whey protein, oat flour and baking powder; mix. Stir in coconut. Drop by tsp. on cookie sheet and bake at 350° for 5 to 6 min. Watch so they don't burn as you are using butter. Makes approximately 5 dozen cookies

Recipe Note: 1 carbohydrate and 2 protein each.

PEANUT BUTTER MELTS

2 sticks butter room temperature
½ c. unsweetened peanut butter
⅔ c. splenda
1 egg

1 c. vanilla whey protein powder
½ c. + 2 tbl. oat flour
1 tsp. baking powder

Cream softened butter, peanut butter and splenda; add egg and mix. Add vanilla whey protein, oat flour and baking powder; mix till blended. Bake at 350° for 5 to 7 min. Watch so they don't burn as you are using butter. Makes approximately 5 dozen cookies.

Recipe Note: 1 carbohydrate and 2 protein each.

PECAN CUP COOKIES

1 c. butter room temperature
½ c. shortening
⅓ c. splenda
2 tsp. molasses
1 egg

1 c. vanilla whey protein powder
½ c. oat flour
1 tsp. baking powder
½ tsp. baking soda

Cream softened butter, shortening, molasses and splenda; add egg and mix. Add vanilla whey protein, oat flour, baking powder, baking soda; mix till blended. Refrigerate ½ hr. and then make into small balls. Make a small indentation in each one and fill with about ½ tsp. of pecan mixture. These spread a lot so leave space. Bake at 350° for 5 to 6 min. Watch so they don't burn as you are using butter. Makes approximately 4 dozen cookies.

Recipe Note: 2 carbohydrates and 2 protein each.

Pecan filling

½ c. find ground pecans
4 tbl. sour cream

1 tsp. molasses
2 tsp. splenda

Mix together all the ingredients. Use in cookies.

SOUR CREAM COOKIES

2 sticks butter room temperature
½ c. shortening
⅔ c. splenda
¼ c. sour cream
1 egg

1½ c. vanilla whey protein powder
½ c. + 2 tbls. oat flour
1 tsp. baking powder
½ tsp. baking soda

Cream softened butter, shortening, and splenda; add egg and mix. Add vanilla whey protein, oat flour, baking powder, and baking soda; mix till blended. Drop by tsp. on cookie sheet; these spread a lot so leave space and bake at 350° for 5 to 6 min. Watch so they don't burn. Makes approximately 5 dozen cookies.

Recipe Note: 1 carbohydrate and 2 protein each.

THUMBPRINT COOKIES

2 sticks butter room temperature
½ c. shortening
⅔ c. splenda
1 egg

1 c. vanilla whey protein powder
½ c. oat flour
1 tsp. baking powder
½ c. ground nuts

Cream softened butter, shortening and splenda; add egg and mix. Add vanilla whey protein, oat flour and baking powder and mix till blended. Refrigerate ½ hour. Put ground nuts in small bowl. Roll dough into small balls and roll lightly in nuts. Press a finger in each one to make an indentation. Bake at 350° for 5 to 7 min. Watch so they don't burn as you are using butter. Makes approximately 5 dozen cookies. Put a dab of frosting in each one. See index for frosting recipes. Refrigerate.

Recipe Note: 2 carbohydrates and 2 protein each.

WALNUT COOKIES

2 sticks butter room temperature
½ c. shortening
⅓ c. splenda
1 egg

1 c. vanilla whey protein powder
½ c. oat flour
1 tsp. baking powder
¾ c. chopped walnuts

Cream softened butter, shortening and splenda; add egg and mix. Add vanilla whey protein, oat flour, baking powder; mix. Stir in nuts. Drop by tsp. on cookie sheet and bake at 350° for 5 to 6 min. Watch so they don't burn as you are using butter. Makes approximately 5 dozen cookies.

Recipe Note: 1 carbohydrate and 2 protein each.

Baking
Low Carb

290631-99

Candy

My Favorite Recipe

_____
_____
_____
_____
_____
_____
_____
_____
_____
_____
_____
_____
_____
_____
_____
_____
_____
_____
_____
_____
_____

Candy

CHOCOLATE PEANUT BUTTER FUDGE

12 tbl. butter
¼ c. peanut butter
1 c. baking cocoa
1 c. heavy whip cream warmed
1 tbl. liquid sweetener Sweet &
  Low

½ c. Splenda
1 tsp. vanilla
½ c. vanilla whey protein powder

Melt butter; mix in peanut butter and stir in baking cocoa. Add warm whipping cream and then stir in liquid sweetener, splenda, vanilla and vanilla whey protein powder. Pour into a 8 x 8 pan lined with wax paper. Keep in freezer. Using wax paper, lift fudge out and cut in to pieces. Keep in freezer or refrigerator.

Recipe Note: 2 carbohydrates and 1.5 protein each.

COCONUT CHOCOLATE CANDY

¾ c. baking cocoa
2 sticks butter
½ c. heavy whipping cream
  warmed
½ c. splenda

1 tsp. vanilla extract
1 tsp. coconut extract
¾ c. ground almonds
1 c. unsweetened coconut

Melt butter and stir in cocoa. Add warm whip cream. Stir in splenda, vanilla extract and coconut extract. Add coconut and almonds. Spread on a 10 x 15 jelly roll pan. Freeze and then cut into 1 x 2 pieces. Keep in freezer.

Recipe Note: 1.3 Carbohydrate and 2.5 protein each.

DARK FUDGE

10 tbl. butter
1½ cup baking cocoa
⅔ c. heavy whipping cream
  warmed
½ c. splenda

1 tbl. liquid sweetener Sweet &
  Low
⅓ c. vanilla whey protein powder
1 c. chopped walnuts

Melt butter; stir in cocoa; mix. Stir in warm whip cream. Add splenda, liquid sweetener, vanilla whey and then nuts. Pour in to a 8 x 8 pan lined with wax paper. Freeze. Lift fudge out with wax paper and cut into 36 pieces.

Recipe Note: 3 carbohydrates and 1 protein each.

GUMMY CANDY

Baking
Low Carb

3 pkgs. unflavored gelatin
½ c. cold water
1 pkg. Kool-Aid

¼ c. splenda
1 tbl.. liquid sweetener Sweet &
Low

Sprinkle gelatin over water and stir. Microwave for 1 minute. Liquid will appear clear. Stir in Kool-Aid, splenda and sweetener. Pour into an 8 inch cake pan. Refrigerate for 5 min and take out of refrigerator and stir to remove bubbles. Put back until solid. Cut into small squares.

Recipe Note: Total carbohydrates 6.

MAPLE WALNUT FUDGE

1 c. butter
⅓ c. heavy whip cream warmed
⅓ c. vanilla whey protein powder
¼ c. splenda

¼ tsp. molasses
3 tsp. maple extract
⅓ c. walnuts

Melt butter; mix with warm whip cream. Stir in vanilla whey protein, molasses, maple extract and splenda. Pour into a 8 x 8 pan lined with wax paper. Put in freezer. When hard, lift out of pan with wax paper and cut into 16 pieces. Keep in freezer.

Recipe Note: Less than 1 carbohydrate and 2 protein each.

290631-99

MINT DELIGHT

2 sticks butter
⅓ c. heavy whip cream warmed
⅓ c. vanilla whey protein powder
¼ c. splenda

1 tsp. mint extract
1 tsp. peppermint extract
green food color

Melt butter; mix with warm whip cream. Stir in vanilla whey protein, splenda and extracts. Add a drop of food color. Pour into a 8 x 8 pan lined with wax paper. Put in freezer.

Second Layer

2 sticks butter
¼ c. baking cocoa
⅓ c. heavy whip cream warmed
⅓ c. vanilla whey protein

¼ c. splenda
1 tbl. liquid sweetener Sweet & Low
1 tsp. vanilla extract

Melt butter and stir in cocoa. Add warm whip cream; mix. Stir in vanilla whey protein, splenda, sweetener and vanilla. Set aside till the mint mixture has set up....about 30 min., in freezer, and then pour this on top and put in freezer. When hard, lift out of pan with wax paper and cut into 16 pieces and keep in freezer.

Recipe Note: 2 carbohydrates and 2 protein each.

PEANUT BUTTER FUDGE

½ c. butter
½ c. unsweetened peanut butter
⅓ c. heavy whip cream warmed
⅓ c. vanilla whey protein powder

¼ c. splenda
1 tsp. vanilla
½ c. chopped walnuts

Melt butter; mix in peanut butter and then warm whip cream. Stir in vanilla whey protein, splenda, vanilla and walnuts. Pour into a 8 x 8 pan lined with wax paper. Put in freezer. When hard lift out of pan with wax paper and cut into 16 pieces and keep in freezer.

Recipe Note: 2 carbohydrates and 2.5 protein each.

Baking
Low Carb

290631-99

This & That

My Favorite Recipe

_____
_____
_____
_____
_____
_____
_____
_____
_____
_____
_____
_____
_____
_____
_____
_____
_____
_____
_____
_____

This & That

CARAMEL PORK RINDS

5 to 6 ounces pork rinds
6 tbl. melted butter
1 tsp. liquid sweetener Sweet &
  Low

2 tbl. splenda
2 tsp. caramel extract
1 tsp. cinnamon

In a bowl combine melted butter, sweetener, splenda, caramel extract and cinnamon; stir till blended. Put pork rinds in a large bowl and pour butter mixture over the top....stir till well coated. Put on a cookie sheet and bake at 300° for 10 minutes. Cool and keep in sealed container.

Recipe Note: Total recipe 5 carbohydrates and 64 protein.

EGGNOG

6 4 oz. containers Egg beaters
2⅓ c. heavy whip cream
⅓ c. water
¼ tsp. vanilla extract
⅓ c. splenda

2 tsp. liquid sweetener Sweet &
  Low
¼ tsp. ground nutmeg
2 tsp. rum extract

Combine egg substitutes, cream, water, splenda, liquid sweetener, vanilla and rum extract and nutmeg. Mix well and refrigerate.

Recipe Note: Each ½ cup serving has 2 carbs. and 5 protein.

EGGNOG COFFEE

1 c. coffee
1 egg yolk
2 tsp. splenda

½ c. cream
dash nutmeg

Mix splenda and egg yolk. Place cream into a saucepan and heat over low setting till warm. Whisk egg mixture into cream and heat till steaming. Pour coffee into two cups and top with egg mixture. Sprinkle with nutmeg.

Recipe Note: 2 carbohydrates per cup.

EUROPEAN COFFEE

1 egg white
1/4 tsp. vanilla extract
1 tsp. splenda

1 tbl. heavy whipping cream
1 tbl. water

Beat egg white until forms soft peaks. Gently add vanilla and splenda; beat till stiff peaks are formed. Place in 2 coffee mugs and pour coffee over egg whites. Mix heavy whipping cream and water together. Top coffee with heavy whipping cream mixture.

Recipe Note: 1 carb. per cup.

LOW CARB CONDENSED MILK

1 1/4 c. heavy whipping cream
3 egg yolks

1/2 c. splenda

Combine whipping cream, yolks and splenda and whisk over a low heat; stirring till thickened. Cool.

Recipe Note: 23 carbohydrates and 9 protein.

MARSHMALLOWS

3 envelopes unflavored gelatin
1/4 c. cold water
3/4 c. boiling water

3 tbl. splenda
3 egg whites

Thanks to Fiona for this one. Sprinkle gelatin over cold water in mixing bowl; set aside for 5 minutes to soften. Add to boiling water in saucepan, cook and stir until gelatin is dissolved. Remove from heat. Cool to consistency of thick syrup. Stir in splenda and vanilla. Beat egg whites into soft peaks. Very slowly, trickle a small stream of gelatin mixture into egg white, beating until all gelatin mixtures is mixed in. Continue beating until light and fluffy. Pour into pan and cut.

Recipe Note: 3 carbohydrates.

290631-99

MEXICAN COFFEE

2 c. water
¼ c. coarsely ground coffee
¼ tsp. molasses

2 tsp. splenda
1 cinnamon stick

Mix water, ground coffee, molasses, cinnamon and splenda in a saucepan. Bring to a boil, reduce heat and simmer for 5 minutes. Strain into 2 mugs.

Recipe Note: 1 carbohydrate per cup.

MEXICAN MOCHA COFFEE

1½ c. strong coffee
2 tsp. baking cocoa
2 tsp. splenda
¾ tsp. cinnamon

¼ tsp. nutmeg
1 tbl. splenda
½ c. heavy whipping cream

Combine coffee, cocoa, 2 tsp. splenda, ¼ tsp. cinnamon and nutmeg; mix. Whip heavy cream, ½ tsp. cinnamon, nutmeg and splenda until soft peaks form. Pour coffee into 4 cups and top with whip cream mixture.

Recipe Note: 1. 5 carbohydrate per cup.

ORANGE SPICE WALNUTS

2 tbl. melted butter
1 tsp. cinnamon
½ tsp. grated orange peel

3 tbl. splenda
1 c. walnuts

Combine butter, cinnamon, orange peel and walnuts; mix. Add splenda; stir until well coated. Put on cookie sheet. Cook at 300° for 10 minutes.

Recipe Note: 16 carbohydrates and 20 protein.

SPICE COFFEE

2 c. water
¼ c. coarsely ground coffee
½ tsp. orange peel

½ tsp. lemon peel
1 cinnamon stick
2 tsp. splenda

Place water, coffee, orange peel, lemon peel, cinnamon stick and splenda in a saucepan. Bring to a boil, reduce heat and simmer 5 minutes. Strain into 2 mugs.

Recipe Note: 1.5 carbohydrate per cup.

SWEET NUTS

Baking
Low Carb

4 tbl. butter
5 tbl. splenda
I tsp. liquid sweetener Sweet &
  Low
I tsp. cinnamon

½ tsp. vanilla extract
½ tsp. caramel extract
2 c. whole almonds or walnut
  halves

Melt butter and stir in sweetener, cinnamon, vanilla extract, and caramel extract. Add nuts, splenda and stir till coated. Spread on a Pam sprayed cookie sheet and bake at 300° for 20 min. Stir after 10 min. Cool.

Recipe Note: 32 carbohydrates and 40 protein.

WHIPPED CREAM TOPPING OR FILLING

I c. heavy whipping cream
I tbl. Splenda

¼ tsp. liquid sweetener saccharin
½ tsp. vanilla

Place cream, splenda, sweetener, and vanilla in chilled bowl. Beat until cream holds shape. Do not over beat or you'll have butter! Makes 2 cups.

Recipe Note: Total carbohydrates 7 and 5 protein.

Cocoa Whip Cream

2 tbls. cocoa

I tbls. splenda

Prepare as for whip cream but add cocoa and an additional tbls. of cocoa.

Recipe Note: Carbohydrate 12 and protein 7.

Pistachio Whipped Cream

½ tsp. almond

½ tsp. vanilla

Prepare as above but add almond extract and change vanilla to I tsp.

Coffee Whipped Cream

I tsp. coffee extract

I tbl. splenda

Prepare as above but add coffee extract and increase splenda to 2 tbl.

290631-99

INDEX OF RECIPES

Cookies

Candy

This & That

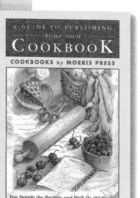

PUBLISH YOUR OWN cookbook

Morris Press Cookbooks has the right ingredients to make a really great cookbook. Write us, call us, or contact us at our web site, and we'll send you our **FREE** step-by-step *Guide to Publishing Your Own Cookbook*. It's so easy.

You Supply
the recipes
& *we'll do*
the *Rest!*™

Three ways to contact us:
- Complete and return the **postage paid reply card** below.
- Order from our web site at **www.morriscookbooks.com**.
- Call us at **800-445-6621, ext. CB**.

NO POSTAGE
NECESSARY
IF MAILED
IN THE
UNITED STATES

BUSINESS REPLY MAIL
FIRST-CLASS MAIL   PERMIT NO. 36   KEARNEY, NE

POSTAGE WILL BE PAID BY ADDRESSEE

Morris Press Cookbooks
P.O. Box 2110
Kearney, NE 68848-9985

III1II1II1I1I1I1II1I1I1I1I1II1I1I1I1I1I